Pat

I know that you have many fond memories of your mother. I hope that when you read this book, it will remind you of her love and devotion to her family.

Love
Janine

Growth In Grandmothering

Growth In Grandmothering

Barbara B. Smith

Bookcraft
Salt Lake City, Utah

Library of Congress Catalog Card Number: 86-72074

ISBN 0-88494-616-9

4th Printing, 1990

Printed in the United States of America

This book is dedicated with love
to my grandchildren
for the joy they have brought to me
and for the limitless possibilities
of their lives

Contents

Acknowledgments

A book like this one cannot come to fruition without extensive sharing of time and self.

If I could I would name all who have contributed, but that would mean listing everyone who has ever had an influence on my life from the time I entered the world until now. I am quite certain that I would forget someone of great significance to me. Still, in my heart I do not forget and I am grateful for all.

I would like to thank all of the Relief Society sisters with whom I have shared conversations about very important things like babies, children, grandchildren, motherhood, and homes. I would like to express appreciation to those wonderful women of American Mother, Inc. and the National Council of Women who have shared with me their experiences in building homes and rearing families. I am grateful to the many friends and business associates who have opened their memories to enrich my thinking about these most fundamental topics.

I would offer here a special appreciation to my husband, my children, their partners, and my grandchildren, who shared with me so graciously the sacred and intimate moments of living upon which this book is based.

This book could not have been completed without the writing and editing help of Moana B. Bennett. She is my friend and my willing, capable consultant, a woman who has always put the work of the Lord first in her life.

Prologue

Frequently the question has been asked of me, "What do you do with all of your spare time now that you have been released as the general president of the Relief Society? Have you gone back to your grandchildren?"

After answering that question "yes and no" over and over again, a question from the Psalms came to my mind. The Psalmist asked the Lord, "What is man, that thou art mindful of him?" (Psalm 8:4). Recently I have begun to ask myself some questions that this scripture brings to mind: Am I more mindful of my grandchildren than I have ever been? What difference does my being their grandmother make in their lives? While serving in my Relief Society calling, did I learn anything that would benefit those who were so much a part of my life at that time and forever—my husband, my children, and my grandchildren? What had I really learned in my life now that I was a grandmother? What influence could I have? And, like the Psalmist, I have wondered who my grandchildren are, that I should be mindful of them.

In contemplating these questions, I recall a very early morning on the first day of December when the doctor came from the delivery room wheeling my daughter on a hospital gurney. He took a squirming white bundle from beside her trembling body and handed it to my son-in-law, saying, "Here is your baby boy. He is fine and healthy. His mother did a super job. Congratulations!"

Our hearts were so full that tears welled up in our eyes. My son-in-law took the baby and said over and over again: "My little son! My little son!"

My daughter leaned up on her elbow when she saw me and said, "Mother, that was hard!" "I know," I responded with a smile. "I never said it wouldn't be."

Her attention was already on her husband. Lillian watched the tender way he held the baby, and she whispered to me with a sigh of happy relief. "Our little boy is safely here, and he is whole and healthy. Mother, I love you. Thank you for giving me life. I have a new level of gratitude and appreciation for it and for you, and I thank you.''

That was how I became a grandmother for the first time. Feelings arose within me not unlike other feelings I had known, but still not quite like anything else. There was the familiar rush of joyful relief to know the new baby was here and whole, augmented by a grateful surge of happiness that Lillian was also safely through the birth. That was a new dimension. Then I felt that rewarding warmth that came with her expression of love and gratitude to me for having given her life. That also was a brand-new, unexpected emotion.

There were smiles and kisses and hugs all around before our happy little entourage proudly paraded out of the doorway of the delivery room and down the long hospital corridor, the happy father and his newborn son leading the parade to the infant nursery. I don't believe I missed a step, even when I realized I had joined an almost endless parade of generations who had gone before me, my proud young son-in-law, my tired but happy daughter, and the newest of all—this small, almost defenseless boy-child.

I thought about a lot of things that night. I thought of birth— not only of my grandson's birth but also the birth of a new mother, a new father, a new grandfather—and then I discovered there was a new grandmother. I was that new person. I had never been a grandmother before. I had been a daughter, a child, a young woman, a sister, a wife, a mother, and many, many more people—such as a secretary, a volunteer—oh, the list is endless. But tonight I was a grandmother for the first time. This birth transformed all of these other people into something new at the precise moment that my first grandchild came into mortality. I liked the transformation. In fact, I liked it a lot. Another new feeling emerged, a feeling of deepest humility as I considered how very thin is the veil between heaven and earth. I knew my daughter would lie awake that night with tears in her eyes as she too contemplated this truth from her new perspective—as a mother for the first time.

I had been looking forward to this birth for a long time with great anticipation. I felt like shouting the good news of this great event to the whole world. But I didn't. I just quickened my step and held high an invisible banner that read, "Happy Birthday, Everyone!" We marched down those hospital halls and stopped in front of the window where babies were sleeping, where babies were crying.

We watched through the window as the nurse took our baby's vital signs, and we marveled at each movement made by this new little person that was instantly such an important part of our lives. A few minutes ago he had been only an object of expectation. Now he was the center of our attention. I thought about the new grandfather who was my partner but who was not standing there by the window looking in at this miracle child. I must call him right away, I thought. He had known it was about time for his first grandchild to be born when he left town to keep his business appointment. He would be anxious tonight. There were others I needed to call—the new great-grandfathers, new aunts, and new uncles. Who was this child that we should all be mindful of him?

When both mother and baby were comfortably situated in their hospital rooms, my son-in-law drove me home. We had always been able to talk freely with each other, this young man and I. That night there was an even sweeter feeling of commonality between us as we discussed his responsibilities as a new father and mine as a new grandmother. We shared our desires, dreams, and fondest hopes.

He said: "Suddenly I understand so many things. I have always wondered why my parents were so protective. I feel that same way now. I would do anything to shield my son from the dangers and hurts of the world."

I got out of the car and he turned the key, started the engine, and drove away. In the quiet night I thought for a moment that I could understand his feelings. In fact, I was confident that I could even predict what shielding his son from the dangers and hurts of the world would be for him. It was harder for me to put into words what it would mean to be a grandmother. I looked into the limitless heavens for a moment before I went into the house. My child had now become a mother. I didn't worry about being a grandmother any more than I had worried about becoming a mother. I think I simply felt that I would know what to do. Women had been doing it for centuries. I would share with my daughter all that I knew about babies. That's what my mother had done for me. When Lillian had been my baby I felt that same very special feeling that comes with each new child. Then I could hold her and feed her and feel the warmth of her little body close to mine. It did seem strange now to be part of a new generation. I wondered if I could do for my daughter and her child any of the good and helpful things which my mother and my mother-in-law had done for me. And I wondered if I could adjust to leaving this baby at night.

That little baby was the first grandchild for both his paternal and his maternal grandparents. He was truly a welcome child. He almost never cried. Everyone wanted to hold him, and perhaps that was the reason he did not cry. Whenever his eyes opened someone was there to pick him up. He was rocked. He was cuddled constantly, first in one set of loving arms and then in another. I don't believe a family could have been happier with a child than we were with him—aunts, uncles, grandparents, great-grandparents, and mother and father, of course. It was pure delight to have this child join our lives. There was a sense of awe. There was simply the great joy of life itself.

I had felt this overwhelming excitement at the joy of life before. It had come with the birth of each of my own children. But the night on which I became a grandmother for the first time I was remembering feelings from a long-ago place, deep in my mind.

As a child I had been taken to Wyoming to spend some time with my grandmother, who was a country doctor. Once while we were there, she had to make an unexpected house call and took my brother and me along. We had been told to stay in the car as she pulled her black bag from behind the front seat of that big Buick and hurried inside. For a while we sat quietly in Grandmother's car, but soon the children of the household coaxed us to come play with them. We did. Our games took us running around the yard and out by the corrals, and then we burst noisily around one corner of the house. There, framed in the old window, I saw my grandmother washing a newborn infant, and, suddenly, as more children's faces crowded the window to get a peek, my grandmother laughed delightedly. She was laughing because of the safe arrival of the baby she was bathing. She was laughing at the window full of children's faces. And she was laughing because of the joy she felt to be so much a part of the coming forth of a new life. Life is a precious gift. She knew it and I knew she knew it. And now, for myself, I too knew it.

The familiar rhythm of my own household soon engulfed me. There were still five children at home. Soon I would know more about becoming a grandmother. I was already overwhelmed by motherhood, and now there would be a new generation. I wasn't sure what the day-to-day demands on a grandmother would be. I wondered how it would all fit together.

Now that I am older and I have more experience in life, I am aware that I have only just begun to understand what an incredible experience life really is. I am no longer the general president of the Relief Society, it is true, but I have not "gone back" to my grandchildren. I am determined to go forward with my children and my grandchildren, sharing what I have learned and learning from them. In my Church service to this point I have learned something of the Lord's eternal truths. In my family experiences I have learned something of human beings and how they grow. I want to have added vision about being a grandmother.

It occurs to me now, at this point in my life, that I am on the threshold of the greatest period of growth in my mortal experience. All else has been a preparation, the gaining of a background. I am what I am. I have my own testimony of Jesus Christ and his teachings. I am a mother. I am a grandmother. The challenge as taught by ancient and modern prophets is to have the courage to live by the teachings of Jesus Christ and thus to shape a life more abundant, more perfect in love.

And who are my grandchildren that I should be mindful of them? They are the individuals through whom I will learn more of life and love than I have known before.

Oh, yes, I tell those who ask, I am going to have all the experiences I can with my grandchildren. I am not going back to my grandchildren so much as going forward with them. I have so much yet to learn. I have only just begun. Of one thing I am certain—there is great growth in being a grandmother.

Ye must grow in grace and in the
knowledge of the truth.

—D&C 50:40

CHAPTER ONE

A New Grandmother:
Green and Growing

In one way it is very easy to define what it means to be a
grandmother. The dictionary gives only one very simple definition: A grandmother is the mother of a child's mother or the
mother of a child's father.

But anyone who has been a grandmother knows that such a
definition is only the beginning. Anyone who has ever been a
grandmother also knows that becoming a grandmother is more
a process that never ends than an act of completion. One of the
most important things a grandmother can possibly do is to recognize that a certain grace can accompany the gradual growth
that takes place during the seasons of her life if she allows the
new experience to be an expanding, changing, maturing, developing period. To resist the changes that will surely come
will bring bitterness and unhappiness. To deny the new insight into fundamental human relationships will abort the
happy possibilities of relationships with the new human being
who confers upon you the title of grandmother.

The word *grandmother* has not traditionally been used as a verb nor does any dictionary define it as such. And yet the experiences that come with the new generation cry out for the dynamic reality of action which a verb brings. One friend wanted me to begin my grandmothering immediately with the active voice of the verb *to brag*. She gave me a "grandmother's brag book" and told me that I should carry it with me at all times. She assured me it would be a great visual aid for the "bragging" that I was entitled to do as a new grandmother. But more than that she wanted me to understand that I should begin recording in pictures and in words the meaningful moments of this new phase of my life with all of its impressions.

I should have taken a picture of my husband when he stepped off of the plane, laden with baby gifts. He had taken the next flight home after he knew his first grandchild had been born. As he walked down the jetway he called, "Where is the baby?" It was almost as if he expected the baby to be there at the airport to greet him. We drove directly to the hospital without even going home first. He had made several long-distance telephone calls to talk with our daughter since the big event. Now he gave this new family his undivided attention. He looked in the nursery window and quickly picked out his grandson. He had been outgoing with his own children, but he was even more so with this firstborn grandchild and said, "It's too bad we didn't have grandchildren first so we'd know more about raising our children." It was fun to meet Doug at the airport that morning and to be a part of his enthusiastic, triumphal arrival at the hospital for his first look at our grandchild.

There is something to be said for the wonderful nonjudgmental love we found ourselves giving this baby. Without any of the pressures and responsibilities of rearing the child, we could simply enjoy him. The expression of this noncritical, undivided love was a new experience, and we were completely captivated. Looking back on the arrivals of thirty-six similar and yet wonderfully unique grandchildren, I now see that love can grow and, in fact, does grow — not by the simple factor of one plus one but actually by infinite factors which multiply beyond measure. It seems to me that a grandmother comes to a better understanding that love cannot be bounded and that the more love she gives away, the more love she has to give.

The day after my daughter gave birth to my first grandchild did not seem so very different from the day before. I remember getting up as usual, perhaps without quite as many hours of sleep during the night as I was used to, but with more enthusiasm for the brightness of that new day made brighter by the expectancy that good things were certain to happen.

But my day also included the usual: getting the children up, fixing breakfast, encouraging the children through their morning chores, and straightening the house. The children were excited when I told them the good news, and they would not be off to school until they had my word that immediately after school they could call the hospital and get a firsthand detailed report about their young nephew—they were anxious to let everyone know that they should be treated with more respect now that they had the new title of uncle or aunt.

One of the first things I did was to call family members and friends. I had to make some calls to complete my Church assignment as a stake spiritual living teacher. Calls came in for Doug, who was then serving as a stake president. Our Church friends were all delighted to know we were first-time grandparents. They excitedly told others, and soon my telephone was constantly ''a-chatter.''

While I did my housework, a plan evolved. I knew then what I wanted to do to help Lillian and her husband, Claron, too. It was something my mother and my mother-in-law had done for me. I had appreciated it very much, and in a way it had become part of my dreams for the future when I, too, would help my daughters with their newborn babies.

As soon as I finished my own chores I would go to Lillian's and begin to get her house ready for her homecoming. My mother and mother-in-law had spent all day cleaning for me with my first baby. They used wallpaper cleaner on the walls; washed woodwork, windows, bedspreads, and curtains; and waxed the floors. Everything was polished and cleaned until it sparkled. I still remembered that clean smell.

I wanted my immaculately clean daughter to come home to such a house so that she would remember that fresh aroma, too, and the love that came with it. Her husband welcomed the idea, since cleaning the house was not part of his training nor inclination, even though he was personally a very neat, tidy, and fastidious person.

I found that being a grandmother was in this way a lot like being a mother. I was doing the things I had seen my mother do. The house was squeaky clean the day Lillian went to the hospital, and I wanted it to be the same for mother and son to come home to from the hospital. I was there at the house waiting. The doorbell didn't even get a chance to ring. I saw them drive into the driveway and opened the door wide to welcome them home. I remember encouraging Lillian to get into bed and rest because coming home from the hospital was excitement enough for one day. Besides, soon there would be visitors—grandfathers, neighbors, and those proud first-time aunts and uncles.

Claron followed her with the baby into the bedroom and put him in my arms. I held him close and reveled in his new-baby smell and kissed him while my tears dropped softly on his blanket. Perhaps it was a sort of grandmother's lullaby I sang as I spoke to him of happy dreams and joyful expectations. The words I had heard President N. Eldon Tanner speak came forcefully to mind: "She [Mother] is a co-partner with God in bringing his spirit children into the world. What a glorious concept! No greater honor could be given. With this honor comes the tremendous responsibility of living and caring for those children so they might learn their duty as citizens and what they must do to return to their Heavenly Father." (*Woman* [Salt Lake City: Deseret Book Company, 1979], p. 6.)

Claron carried in vases and pots of flowers and some of the darling little baby-boy gifts of clothing which had arrived at the hospital. Soon Claron went back to school. Lillian and I began to talk about her hospital experience and about the birth of the baby. She had many questions: "What can I expect of my new baby? What? What? What if? What do you think, Mother?" On another morning not so long before, my own mother had answered my questions in such a setting; it interested me that they were mostly the same questions.

"You have a fine, healthy, normal baby," I told her. "He just wants to be fed when he is hungry, changed and made dry when he is wet, kept clean, given a bath at least once each day, rubbed down at night, and comforted when he cries. You can do all of those things."

"Yes," she replied confidently. "I can."

"At first your baby will consume every minute of the day," I told her, "but it doesn't take many weeks before you get the baby on a routine and you can fit the other things you want to do into your day." That was reassuring, she said.

"Mother," she asked, "will you give my baby his first bath?" I was pleased, and like my mother before me I prepared the bath, took the baby to the warm water, and showed my daughter how I bathed my babies. It started a lovely tradition which I have enjoyed with my daughters. For the first few days I took care of Lillian's house and served her meals in bed when she wanted them and helped her with the baby.

The sweet interludes at Lillian's home with the brand-new baby were joyful. I hope I brought her the comfort and the peace my mother had given to me. Soon she was strong enough to take over her own home.

To me these details help define, as much as anything else, what it means to be a grandmother. It means to share through conversation, through instruction, through example, through coaching, and through encouragement all the wisdom learned from one's own parents and from one's own experience so that the new mother will have the confidence to care for her new child. For me it was a joyful experience to see my daughter become a mother. In that natural transition of which I was an observer and also a participant, I realized that I had become a grandmother.

I believe the first major contribution I made to my grandchild was to his parents. I aspired to be a helping hand, and I believe I was. I was quite certain that most of the significant contributions that a grandmother can make are in the nature of "on-the-job training" of the newborn's mother and father; after all, my daughter had been a daughter for over twenty years, but a mother for only a few days. I knew that I should share any part of the knowledge I had about caring for and nurturing infants that my children might want—for at that moment I knew much more of life and love than they did. I wanted always to be a source of unconditional, pure love. I wanted my children to know I was waiting there to help, to listen, to love in any circumstance. I felt certain I would always be able to rejoice in the growth and accomplishments of my daughter's child. I knew I didn't have the responsibility of discipline, and it seemed easy enough to transmit my joy in the perfect new life that had been entrusted to my daughter's care and keeping. It would be exciting to begin new family traditions and extend them through our lives with this first grandbaby and all of our future grandchildren.

I'm not certain who was the most delighted in the family when the children first saw the new baby, but I do know that neither the sons nor the daughters could keep from touching his soft cheeks or the tiny little fingers that closed tightly about theirs. They all adored him and stood close by hoping he would wake up and need them to hold him.

A few days after Lillian had come home, Doug's father called and asked if we would take him to visit the newest member of his posterity. He had a package in his hands when we picked him up. When he walked into Lillian and Claron's rented home, he expressed his approval and then said, "I thought it was time I became acquainted with my newest great-grandchild." Lillian picked the sleeping baby up from the bassinet and handed him to her grandfather. He exchanged the gift for the baby. As he sat down in the big overstuffed chair and looked into the baby's eyes, he said, "Grandma Winnie was so pleased when you told her that you were expecting this baby. She immediately called our ward Relief Society president and ordered a baby quilt for it. The Relief Society sisters brought it over after Grandma Winnie passed away, and I have been keeping it for you. It is an expression of her love to you and to him. I will always think of her when I look at him. Thank you for letting me have this moment." He handed the baby back to his granddaughter, and there was a tenderness shared between them which we will never forget.

In such remarkable moments I have come to recognize that one element of becoming a grandmother has to do with maintaining the soft and loving bands that connect the generations and hold families together. In a larger sense I am aware that children and grandchildren are intended to provide bonds of love which connect each of us to a loving Heavenly Father. That they are connecting links is more visible to me now that I am a grandmother, perhaps because it is easier now to step gracefully back from the daily urgencies and catch a fleeting glimpse of the truth regarding the grand vistas of life.

Behold thou hast a gift, and blessed art
thou because of thy gift. Remember it is
sacred and cometh from above.
— D&C 6:10

CHAPTER TWO

Growing Through Diversity

As a mother I was aware that children were blessed with certain gifts which made them unique and different. But this understanding has been greatly enlarged as thirty-six individuals have joined our family ranks.

When my children were at home, I felt a certain responsibility to treat them equally as I directed the daily routines of the household. The fact that each child became a part of that routine focused my attention on their similar needs and only from time to time on their differences.

But with grandchildren there is time and distance, and one becomes acutely aware of the wonderful diversity in size, in talent, and in attitude toward life. Some of our grandchildren are redheads, some have dark eyes and dark hair, and some are blond and blue-eyed. The mixture of genes has infinite variety, and the world of a grandmother is decidedly more exciting because of it.

It is not only in size and shape, however, that one finds diversity. The differences in abilities and even in capabilities of grandchildren help those who love them to develop greater understanding, appreciation, tolerance, and even an acceptance of truth.

Julie came to us with a God-given gift and a desire to sing. She was imitating her mother's singing at just nine months, but it was on Mother's Day three years later when she performed in a Sunday School program that her extraordinary talent first publicly manifested itself.

Her grandfather and I were there in the congregation with her mother and father. We all hoped she would perform as practiced and not become frightened. But she was only three years old and we were very nervous.

Then her turn came. She sang so sweetly and so clearly—an unexpected and wonderful surprise. No one in that whole congregation was prepared for the flawless performance she gave. In fact, the conducting officer was so taken with her that he asked her to sing it one more time, and she sang just as loudly and clearly as the first time.

We were all so thrilled and happy. We sat there in tears. We knew she had a gift and wondered what she would do with it. As her grandmother I could hardly wait to show her off. At Christmas time she learned a song about a doll that wanted to be purchased for Christmas. "Shake me I rattle, squeeze me I cry. Please take me home and love me." I was captivated by her each time she sang and was very pleased to take her home and love her.

Perhaps at first our happiness over her gift arose as a sense of joy and pride born of familial ties. But her ability to sing increased and her willing spirit cloaked her talent with a graciousness that made her a favorite whenever she sang. There was something so innocent and so lovely in the tones of her voice that she gave to her audiences a genuine pleasure—a lift of the spirit. She sang at nursing homes for Christmas programs undertaken in the spirit of love and service; she sang with her school classes; she sang in church. And, of course, as she sang she developed her talent. One of our city's outstanding vocal teachers promised her that with just two years of training she would have a voice that could do great things. Julie, of course, would have to give concentrated effort; but, her teacher told her, it would be worth every moment that she gave to develop her God-given gift.

The training of a child's individual talents has to begin with the parents and their loving awareness. I knew that, but I also realized that from time to time I would be able to provide her with other opportunities to perform (thereby encouraging her), including wider audiences who might never otherwise have the chance to hear her sing. One night I was asked to talk about my family and the genealogical records we kept. I decided to project on a large screen overhead transparencies of some family group sheets, and when I talked about Julie I would have her perform. I wanted to make the names on those sheets come alive. I believe it happened for the audience. I know it did for me.

When I look at Julie I remember that "gifts come from God, for the benefit of the children of God" (D&C 46:26). Julie has shared her gift with many.

As I became a grandmother again and again, I began to see that my Heavenly Father was trying to teach me more about the individuality of his children and the gifts he had given freely to them to help them grow to be more like him. I knew I must not take the talents of any grandchild lightly, but help them, each one, to develop and use them so they would be ready to further his work. In fact, I felt an urgency to find ways to help them understand that, as Ralph Waldo Emerson put it: "Talent for talent's sake is a bauble and a show. Talent working with joy in the cause of universal truth lifts the possessor to new power as a benefactor." (*International Dictionary of Thoughts* [Chicago: J. G. Ferguson Publishing Company, 1969], 705.)

Part of the diversity one observes as a grandmother comes from the fact that the training each grandchild receives is enriched by concepts brought from homes other than her own. As her own children impart to grandchildren training in the traditions of her own home, their partners also bring to this important work the traditions they learned in their homes. I know more about the strength of diversity now than I ever knew as a mother.

This realization came to my mind when I offered to keep

Sherilynn's two little girls, Elisa and Melissa, overnight. Her third baby was only two weeks old, and I thought letting them sleep over might give her some much needed rest. The younger of the two was quickly tucked in bed and sound asleep. The four-year-old looked around and saw dishes to be done and food to be put away and straightening up that needed my attention. Noting that two of my older granddaughters were there to help, she asked, "Well, Grandma, what do you want me to do?" My reply was that she should probably go right to bed like her sister. She said, "Oh, no, Grandma, I want to help." She identified the job she would do. "I'll rinse the dishes and you can put them in the dishwasher." She did. She rinsed every dish and every glass and every piece of silver and handed them to me. When the dishes were all in the dishwasher and the pots and pans were rinsed clean, she asked, "Now what do you want me to do? Shall I dust for you?"

The sweet part of that experience was that as she worked she sang, "Where Love Is, There God Is Also." I marveled at that little girl and thought how exciting life would be if all of us could cultivate that wonderful positive attitude in all of the tasks we undertake. How I hoped that the hard tasks of her life would be undertaken with that same happy enthusiasm all the days of her life.

I began to see that a grandmother needs not only to be appreciative of the unique abilities of each grandchild, but also to graciously accept their offerings and thereby help them develop their talents. It might be just a word of encouragement. I have talked to grandmothers who send a note or a single flower with a message of appreciation.

Many grandparents tell me that they are interested enough in the development of a grandchild's talents that they record on film, tape, or video a performance and then arrange a family sharing-time. Endless possibilities open to me, and it has been mind-stretching to contemplate the tremendous influence the children now have in my life. I long to enrich their lives as much as they are enriching mine.

The scriptures have greater application now with so many lives to consider as I read them. I begin to understand passages and examples with a vision made more clear by the deeper diversity of my experience now that I am a grandmother.

I do not often think of my grandchildren as a group; mostly I think of them one by one. As soon as each one has a name and a face, then their uniqueness becomes clear.

I think of Justin. He is just about the cutest little boy ever, and he is "little." All of his cousins of the same age tower over him, but that is only in physical stature. Inside his small frame there is a giant of a young man. He acts and thinks with a maturity beyond his years. He dresses like a little man. He tries to act like a little man. One conversing with him hears intelligent, thoughtful comments and reasonable requests, often far beyond his four years.

One of Justin's great gifts, I have discovered, is his love of performing for the family. He is always willing to stand before them to sing a song or recite a poem or tell a story. He is always smiling. Once his smile got in the way of his performing. His smile was so wide that he could not be understood; he just couldn't form the words. His father took him to one side and explained that if he did not smile so broadly we would understand him better. He tried to control the smile. He even put both hands up to his mouth to hold the smile down but couldn't do it. Finally he went to his father and said: "Dad, you'd better try to wipe this smile off. I've tried and I can't make it go away." The giant spirit and the cheerful, smiling attitude of this "little" boy has given me a new insight into the oft-repeated comment that it is not the size of the body that matters, but only the size of the heart and mind.

Some children wear well the responsibility of being a first-born son. Nathan is one of these. He was calm and gentle as a baby, and those characteristics have stayed with him. The oldest of the six boys in his family, he has been a wonderful example to them. It is a great blessing to a family when the oldest child sets an example of obedience. His choosing to do things which encourage growth and a positive attitude has set a great example for his younger brothers to follow. It is an unusual talent of great worth.

Interestingly enough, as grandparents we can step back and appreciate the simplest form of diversity. When we had our own children at home, busy with all their competitive experiences, we sometimes failed to appreciate the little things that matter so much and give great enrichment. We seemed to be more concerned about other people and what they thought than about individuals and what they did. Then our vision was often limited to the accomplishments that could be seen by men. Grandparents have lived long enough to put each value in a better perspective and to know that the spirit is not limited to physical accomplishments. It is the attitude that leads to greatness, whether it be in the quiet example of a calm and good spirit or in the cheerful, positive attitude so necessary to happiness.

The interesting thing is that grandmothers are blessed with new understanding that allows them to accept a grandchild pretty much as is and to love and cherish each one. Then comes the blessing: They judge not the child by comparison with someone else but see instead the great possibilities within each grandchild.

Joshua is one grandchild who has shown enormous growth and possibility. Before he started school his father decided to teach him the Articles of Faith. He wanted to know just how difficult they were for children to memorize for their advancement from the Primary. So each family home night his parents taught him one article of faith. The fourth was hard for him. He didn't have it memorized by bedtime, so his mother said, "Go to bed now, Joshua, and we'll work on the fourth article of faith again tomorrow." Joshua went, but whenever his parents checked on him during the night, there was that little fellow trying to recite the right words. By morning he delightedly exclaimed, "I've got it. I've got it. I can say the fourth article of faith." And he did. He continued on until he had learned nine articles of faith. One day Joshua came with me as I ran an errand to President Spencer W. Kimball's home. I knew Joshua had learned nine articles of faith, so I said, "Joshua, if President Kimball is home perhaps you could say your nine articles of faith for him." He said, "Why? He knows them, doesn't he?" I had to laugh, and as I did President Kimball answered the door. I told him what I was laughing about. He listened and then said, "Well, Joshua, will you say the nine articles of faith for me?"

Joshua did. He didn't make a single mistake, and President Kimball said, "Joshua, when you have learned all thirteen articles of faith, will you come back and say them all to me?'' Joshua told his parents about the invitation and worked doubly hard to learn the rest of the Articles of Faith.

At a group meeting I attended, President Kimball told about the experience and said, ''By the way, I do know the Articles of Faith. I learned them when I was a little boy milking cows. I always took something with me to memorize. The Ten Commandments, the hymns of the Church, the Articles of Faith, or something that would be faith promoting.''

When I recounted that message to Joshua's parents, they decided to teach that four-year-old child the Ten Commandments as well, and also the song ''We Thank Thee, O God, for a Prophet.'' He learned all of these things in addition to the thirteen Articles of Faith before they took him to recite them again for the prophet. It was a happy day when he went to the office and performed for him. President Kimball then said, ''Joshua, I am proud of you. Now, when you have memorized the New Testament, come back again.''

I took Joshua with me to the Missionary Training Center on many occasions because I wanted those young men to see that they could learn the missionary discussions, the Articles of Faith, and whatever else they were given to do. The scriptures say a little child shall lead them, and those missionaries were led to fortify their resolve as they saw what a four-year-old child could do. They were always impressed as they listened to Joshua recite. Because he was nervous, Joshua always sat down with a big sigh when he finished, but he loved being there with the missionaries.

His brother Jared, on the other hand, did not really enjoy the performing spotlight. Sometimes Jared would forget the words, and sometimes he was just plain miserable when asked to perform. Jared found he had a different talent. In the quiet of his own room he began to sculpt with clay. He seemed almost to withdraw from the outside world and became alive in the quiet work with his hands and the wonderfully malleable clay. His careful observation and insight made it possible for him to create animals and figures of many kinds.

While his family was fascinated by his new-found interest and his creations, his teacher at school began to be very concerned because he spent so much of his free time doing art work and removing himself from the association of the other students. After some discussion it was determined that Jared should use his talents to enhance the classroom and the lessons that would be taught in February on Abraham Lincoln and George Washington.

He went home excited and began working right away. He sculpted a bust of Washington and then attempted to do the whole figure of Abraham Lincoln because he was fascinated by the creases in Lincoln's pants.

When he took his work to school, the boys wanted to hold it and look at it. Jared tried to keep his sculptures from the boys because none of them had been fired and he knew the pieces could be easily broken.

The teacher insisted that he share his creations with his classmates. Jared's fears were realized as he watched his peers push and squeeze his cherished figures. Soon the clay was left lifeless. When he complained, the teacher told him that the students hadn't realized how important the sculptures were to him and that there was nothing that could be done about the damage. "There's something I can do about it. I'll take care of it myself," Jared said, and in one angry gesture he formed the clay back into a ball and threw it into the waste basket. The hours and hours of work were gone, and he went to his desk heartbroken, completely unable to understand the thoughtlessness of both his fellow students and his teacher.

His gift with clay and his sensitive awareness of colors, shapes, forms, and the world around him will be both a joy and a sorrow to him. The insensitivity of some to his gift has already been and will probably yet be painful.

Another truth I have learned about diversity is that some talents are not admired. Thus, one of the significant things a grandmother can do is to comfort a child when hurt and show forth, as the scriptures teach, an abundance of love in genuine appreciation of his unique talents.

It is in recognizing and coming to appreciate the unique qualities of each of my many grandchildren that growth has come to me as a grandmother. I no longer expect them to respond as my children, their parents, responded. Making this transition has required a real stretching of my heart and mind. Slowly but surely, a grandmother begins to push back the sides of her heart to include in a variety of ways the unique gifts that are individual in nature, remembering that each human soul is of great worth. Now I think I know more about the simple truth that each child is sacred; he or she is a child of God.

In so many ways grandmothering is a natural expansion of one's mothering role. The cleaning, the cooking, the nurturing and the loving—even the giving of counsel and advice—these are the natural extensions of one's love. One learns to be more efficient with time management and more effective in human relationships. The real enrichment comes by schooling oneself to accept and genuinely to appreciate diversity. After the first steps, excitement and enrichment accompany the differences.

But of even more significance is the deepening of one's love and appreciation for the great many magnificent individuals who come as grandchildren as their developing lives and talents expand ours. Each one helps us see more clearly that the children of the Lord given to our care and keeping bring us to understand the gospel more fully.

My people must be tried in all things, that
they may be prepared to receive the glory
that I have for them.
                    —D&C 136:31

CHAPTER THREE

Growing Through Adversity

Like many people in this world, I have always hoped nothing
bad would ever happen to me or to mine. However, I have
come to realize that life is often as the Scottish archbishop of
the mid-1600s, Robert Leighton, observed: "Adversity is the
diamond dust heaven polishes its jewels with."

A lot of growing inside has led me to this conviction. Fortunately, the growing season for people is very long, and unlike the growing season for plants, it is continuous.

It is difficult to pinpoint my first encounter with adversity.
Furthermore, it is often difficult to determine just what adversity really is.

I remember conversations with my husband's grandmother
about this subject. I knew that she had two children when her
husband was called to go to England on a mission. He had no
money to leave for the expenses she would have. There were
no funds available to support him in the mission field, either.
But the call came and he felt the obligation to accept it. He was
a man of great faith. Through the generous offer of his wife's

stepfather, who said he would be happy to have Alice and her two little girls come and live in his home, it became possible for him to go. Times were not easy for anyone in those late 1800s, and Alice didn't expect much. It wasn't until years later that she explained how difficult it had been to live under those circumstances.

She and the girls stayed in their assigned room most of the time. A small amount of food was brought to them, just barely enough for the girls, so Alice went without food day after day.

A proud woman, she accepted her plight as necessary and looked back often, knowing that she had successfully struggled through one of the hard times of her life. We marveled at her strength. We thought of her with admiration and hoped that if similar tests came we would endure as she did.

Our turn has come more than once and in different ways. Fortunately, each encounter with adversity has blessed our lives with deeper understanding; but adversities do not come wrapped in equal, readily identifiable packages. Blessings come only after the struggle. It is not as if we had our choice to pay a certain price for a desired measure of personal growth. Growth comes only if our spirits remain teachable during profound hardship. This truth may not be discernible before the fact of suffering.

When December was announced as the month our son Blaine and his wife, Becky, would have their first child, I was elated. December was always a time of hustle and bustle in preparation for Christmas. Still, with all the traditional and beautiful expressions of love that come in December, it seemed to me to be a perfect time for them to bring forth a firstborn child.

The Prophet Joseph Smith had been born in December. We have no familial relationship with him, just profound love for the gospel he has restored. We did and still do feel a very sweet relationship with this man named Smith.

Claron, our first grandchild, had been born in December, as were my mother and grandmother. In my mind December birthdays always meant happy family gatherings.

Of course, there is also the great birthday—the birthday of our Lord and Savior.

So it was about the middle of December when a late-night telephone call came from Blaine: "This is it! We are on our way to the hospital."

We joined Blaine and Becky in the labor room, and our excitement mounted as we waited for the blessed event to occur. In my thoughts I kept comparing Becky with Mary, the mother of Jesus. I suppose it was because my preparations for our annual Christmas program were well under way and because the scriptures focus on Mary and the birth of Jesus. I am a woman who easily relates to that wondrous time when Mary was told that she was "highly favoured" among women and that she would give birth to the Son of God.

I thought that Mary, like Becky, had probably been unaware of the problems she would face because of that magnificent event or of the grave responsibility that would be hers to teach and guide the child through his formative years. Mary would help guide him to an understanding of the powers to which he was entitled and to an acceptance of who he was and what a great work he was sent to accomplish.

Mary may have thought only of the privilege that was hers. She may not have realized that her son, the beloved Son of God, would be ridiculed, demeaned, and crucified. On that first Christmas night so long since past, Mary must have held in her tired but happy arms the infant whom she would call "Jesus" as she had been commanded, and she must have thought, "What a beautiful child I have." The shepherds came and told of the heavens' opening to announce the birth, and the Wise Men came with gifts for the newborn king. An angel soon warned Joseph and Mary to flee with their child to Egypt. The scriptures say Mary pondered all these things in her heart as she met the day-to-day problems of helping her son grow up strong.

Of course, Becky would not face the same challenges, but I was confident that she was a capable enough young woman to assume whatever responsibility came with the care of her baby, no matter what demands might be made on her.

I listened for the cry of the baby. It didn't really matter whether it was a boy or a girl, even though we waited breathlessly for our son to make that big announcement. As always we just hoped that the baby was whole and the mother was doing well.

When Blaine stepped out into the hall where we were gathered, he said, "We have a baby boy!"

Then he unwrapped the baby and let us see his beautiful new son. And he *was* beautiful, with a fair, pink complexion and red hair. But my euphoria ended abruptly when I saw his feet. It was immediately evident that something was terribly wrong with them: they were malformed and twisted.

My reverie ceased. I asked about his feet.

The doctor said, "Only a specialist can tell you about the extent of the malformation." The baby's mother added hopefully, "My mother said my feet were twisted when I was born."

The prayer of my heart was that every blessing possible would come to this child and to his parents—and to his grandparents, too—to help us all meet this new challenge.

Over and over again the doctor's words went through my mind: "Only a specialist can tell you about the extent of the malformation." I tried to hide my anxiety but wished with all my heart that they would call in a specialist that very minute in order to give the baby every chance to grow up with full use of his legs and feet.

There was never any doubt in my mind that this added responsibility given to the parents would be well handled. They would give loving direction to that child through each year, with all of the tenderness and nurturing care he would need to achieve a maturity founded in light and truth. He would be taught to discern the laws of heaven and earth and be ready to direct his own life. I knew that and I thought that he really was a fortunate baby in this respect. Still, would he ever be able to run and play? Would he be able to dribble the ball as his father had done in so many basketball games? What would his father, who loved athletics, think about a boy who couldn't run?

I knew that my son had accepted other difficult experiences uncomplainingly, and I knew he wanted to lead out in righteousness in his new home. He had been taught to accept all callings from the Lord, and this one in connection with his fatherhood would be no exception. I knew he and his family would have the blessings of the most powerful force in the world, the power through which the world and life itself was created—the priesthood of God—to sustain and help them.

Still, I went home pondering. Why?

Why? But suddenly I knew that "why" was a useless question. I must not wallow in the anxiety that descended on me at the first sight of our grandchild's abnormally developed legs and feet; rather, I must trust in the Lord and try to determine what help I could give. As I worked at this change, I began to see a number of miracles occur.

There was the miracle of the child himself. He was a child with an unusually sweet spirit. Through all the challenges of his surgery and his difficulty in getting around, he was patient, cooperative, diligent, and very persistent. From him I learned more about standing firm and going forward resolutely. I became aware that to act repeatedly as directed in order to accomplish a goal was very fundamental to any achievement. I really never knew how grand an achievement it is to learn to walk until I watched my grandson master this ordinary miracle.

Then there was the miracle of his mother and father. They loved him without reservation and were compassionate in providing for him the special help he needed. In my heart I knew that this was a source of sadness for my son, who had loved to participate in athletics both as a growing boy and as a young man. But the prospect that David might not be able to walk or run at the same pace as his friends only seemed to make Blaine more determined that his son should have every opportunity to live as normal a life as possible. Even before David could walk, Blaine took his little boy outside, teaching him how to catch and throw a ball. Eventually he was able to go through little league football, basketball, and baseball. His dad taught him to think as he played and to use his mind and his quickness to offset any hindrance he might feel because his legs were held tight in braces. He may never become a professional ballplayer, but then again he might—thanks to the miracle of modern medicine and the strength of a determined spirit. David has learned to play hard, not to give up, and to reach for the stars.

Through David I learned to feel deeply and understand the ecstasy of achievement for those who struggle with handicaps. Learning with David has been a growing experience for me.

Unfortunately, this was not the only challenge we have had to face with congenital defects among our grandchildren. Words like "defects" and "deformities" carry such heavy burdens that it is hard to write about them. There are the problems of malfunctioning body parts. There are the pains of not being accepted. There are the looks of pity and abhorrence to deal with.

Fortunately, there are also the joys of achieving against the most difficult odds and the tender feelings which come from those who truly love.

In the case of Trent we had to face what was at first an un-detected problem. He had a difficult time keeping his food down. He looked so sad all the time. There was never the ready smile which most well-cared-for infants have. One day his mother decided to have his stomach x-rayed to see if something was wrong; it was obvious to her that his little body was not functioning normally.

The tests proved negative as far as his stomach was con-cerned, but they revealed that his hip sockets were not fully formed. We were very fortunate to discover this malformation early because, had it gone undetected, it might have left him unable to walk or rendered him handicapped for the rest of his life.

The baby had to be put in a body cast. His little face still registered pain and unhappiness. It was a happy day for the whole family when he seemed better and was able to tolerate food. Very slowly his bones began to show improvement, and we noted that the loving care given to him brought a radiance to his whole being.

After a number of months, his mother asked me to tend him while she and her husband went out of town for a few days. I could not believe how hard it was to care for the needs of a baby in a full body cast, with the added weight and inconvenience when I tried to change him or even just hold him to comfort him. When he looked up at me with his deep blue eyes that ex-pressed the misery he was experiencing, I determined that no matter how hard it was I would try to give him a little more pleasure than he might know otherwise. I understood a little more about pain and problem solving than I had before.

My heart went out to him and to every mother who has ever endured a similar hardship. My soul was stretched with love for all of those who care for little ones under such difficult constraints, whether in a home, a pediatric hospital, a center for crippled children, a shelter—whoever or wherever they might be. I now felt a refinement, a purifying spirit, a compassion, and an empathy for others that was beyond anything I had ever learned in happier moments.

Thoughts of the Savior and his love for little children flooded my mind. His love for them became more clear. It was an added incentive to help the child in my arms achieve a little more peace. As I did, a peace beyond my understanding came to me.

One of the most difficult problems to deal with is a congenital deformity. There is a tendency to blame oneself for any problem experienced by a newborn baby. Doug and I had to deal with this when our eldest son called to tell us that four-year-old Daniel had inherited the same problem with his hands and arms that his grandfather, Doug, had. A few years later we discovered that Daniel's brother Andrew also had this congenital problem. Like their grandfather, neither boy could turn his hands palmside up. They had inherited a condition wherein the ulna and radius bones were fused together.

Unlike David's problem, this was not immediately visible and recognizable. But it was nothing to laugh about either. I had lived with Douglas for forty-five years, and I knew how distressed he felt and how difficult certain common, everyday activities had been for him. Simple tasks like catching a baseball, carrying groceries, taking change from a store clerk, and turning a key in a lock had always been painful and inconvenient. Douglas had always preferred not to talk about the problem.

One doctor had told Doug that there were very few such cases in medical history. "I can operate," he said, "but you might find matters worse, and you might lose the use of your arms." Now we had two grandsons with the same problem, facing a lifetime of embarrassment and difficulty if they did not learn to deal with it early.

So the boys' grandfather, Douglas, took charge of the situation. Each time he saw Daniel and Andrew he would play a

game with them to see who could turn his hands over the far-
thest. Sometimes Daniel would ask, "Grandpa, how do you
open the door of the car?" Then his grandfather would take him
out to the car and show him how he does it. He gave Daniel and
Andrew the practice and confidence that, even though they do it
in an unusual way, they can manage the task. Doug knew that
he had conquered the problems his condition had created, and
he knew that his grandsons could, too, if given time and encouragement. But he also felt determined to be their mentor.

As a grandmother I watch them play together. I listen as
Douglas answers their questions, and I also try to help them and
their parents learn different ways to do common tasks. Patiently
he goes over the matters time and time again. As I watch I see
the opening of one heart to another. They share a common
problem, but their solutions are common to each other, too.
When Douglas gives them help, they seem to realize that they
can go on to new accomplishments. They have developed skills
and confidence. They know their grandfather understands,
and they know his condition did not stop his progress. They
know their grandparents do not believe it will stop their
progress, either—we have told them so.

Doug had always felt it best to conceal his ossified arms, but I
had always believed this was a great injustice to himself. Now
he is more open. Most of all, his grandsons know that their problem need not stop their growth in the ultimately more significant
areas of the Spirit. Their grandfather has served valiantly in the
Church in many callings. They can see he is a very good father
and grandfather. They know he has very good business judg-
ment. I do not believe they despair.

Having a physical problem is not a disgrace. Sometimes
having a physical problem opens the mind and heart to significant new thinking and considerable creative achievement.

Five-year-old Curtis needed to wear glasses. His teacher in
preschool had noticed that his eyes crossed as he did close work
at the desk. She suggested he be taken to an ophthalmologist,
who prescribed glasses. We were inclined to think of this new
development as an adversity, but Curtis would have none of our
pity.

For Curtis his new glasses were a mark of distinction. Everybody needs something to help him stand out from the crowd, and glasses made Curtis feel particularly handsome. Because of his positive approach, his friends became admirers. Curtis wore them proudly to preschool, indoors and outdoors, reading or playing games. His admirers included not only his friends but also his parents — with happy sighs — and his grandparents and other members of his extended family.

His new glasses let him explore everything. We had been afraid that they would be a hindrance, but with his positive, boundless spirit he accepted the glasses as a passport to worlds he could not know without them. He readily and willingly made such a wholesome adjustment to his glasses that we could only wonder at his achievement.

I suppose that if I learned nothing else from this child, it was to accept those things that cannot be changed and to do so with the graceful strength that allows one to walk with courage, fortitude, and even triumphant faith.

Through these experiences I have reached a new level of personal faith. I hope it will give me the strength to conquer whatever life requires of my family and me in enduring to the end. Some trials are harder than others, but this much I know: an acceptance of and a personal plan to overcome problems can call forth strength one never thought existed.

In their affliction they will seek me early.
—Hosea 5:15

CHAPTER FOUR

Growing Through Affliction

We are learning as grandparents that accepting an affliction is not disgraceful, and more than that, within our family circle we have seen a joyful growth of love and helpfulness toward one another because of our trials. Until trials came, I didn't know that one could talk about them openly with others and be understood. I didn't understand how close a grandparent could be to a grandchild until that concerned companionship developed with the challenges of a disease or an accident. Challenges do come to a family of many grandchildren in numerous ways.

In a way, I knew how Douglas felt as I heard the doctor announce after studying the X rays and examining our grandson Ben's legs and hips, "It is Perthes disease." It didn't take him long to make the diagnosis. He was certain it was Perthes disease, a deterioration of the hip sockets to the point that the ball of the hip slips from the socket and causes excruciating pain. There had been some related problems in my family.

The doctor continued. ''It is much easier to treat and cure younger children than those who are like Ben, seven years old, almost eight. We are never certain of the outcome with the older children, but we will do all we can.''

He suggested immediate surgery. He told us that Ben would have to be in a body cast over his hips and legs and that he would be very uncomfortable. The doctor was right. Ben was very uncomfortable. His legs ached so much that at times he could hardly stand the unnatural positioning of the hip bones. As the days passed he tried to get up on crutches. They were new to him, and they were painful. He cried as he tried to get around—but he persisted. The cast was so cumbersome that he struggled just to learn how to manage it through doorways and get from one end of the long hall to the other. Each time I looked at him I remembered when my sister had been badly hurt on a toboggan and had to have a full body cast. She never complained, but it was months before her break healed and she could walk again. I really hurt for Ben. He was a determined little boy, and when he found it difficult to get around with crutches he would sit down and scoot himself along while lifting the cast with his arms. He amazed us with the dexterity he developed and the muscles that began to form in his arms. The many hours passed away as he put model airplanes together. He read a lot of books, watched television, and had the school home-teaching service.

We all waited for the day the cast was to be changed. He had already had his eighth birthday, and the doctor permitted his parents to have him carried into the waters of baptism. After the service they went directly to the doctor's office to have Ben recasted. The doctor examined him and then said thoughtfully, ''Ben, I believe I am going to let you try to manage without the cast for a few months and then see how your hips are progressing.''

That decision, we knew, was a direct answer to many prayers in Ben's behalf.

On his first day back at school, he was struggling to get down the stairs when a boy ran past and brushed into him. The push he received was just enough to send him flying down to the bottom of the stairway. Ben tried hard not to cry but could not hold the tears back; the pain was excruciating, and the feared damage had been done. Back to the doctor Ben went. Fortunately, the doctor found that even though there had been some damage, it was minimal. We were all relieved and grateful.

Ben's problem kept reminding me of others in our family who had suffered leg problems. My father's leg was amputated, and he had to learn to walk all over again. His work had forced him to stand most of his life. Varicose veins developed that did not allow the blood to circulate adequately through his body. When his leg was taken off, Dad tried to walk with crutches, but time after time he fell because he could not learn right away to compensate for the loss of the weight of his right leg. But he would get up and try again, even though he was almost eighty years old when the amputation became necessary to save his life.

An aunt of mine developed a diseased leg bone while in training to be a nurse. She had to quit nursing, a profession she dearly loved. The attending doctors wanted to remove her leg, but my doctor grandmother said, "No, you may scrape the bone as much as you think necessary, but for now you must leave her leg on." They did, and though the bone was smaller in that leg than in the other, she was always able to get around. When it seemed to be weakening she took up swimming. At first she was frightened because she didn't know how to swim, but at length she learned and found it wonderful therapy for her leg and for her body. At seventy-five years of age she learned a new skill and gained a measure of good health.

Ben joined David in learning that they had to work for the joy of getting around—something most people never have to learn. But something happens to those who must struggle for things that others take for granted. Something also happens to those who love and watch the struggle and pray.

There is a depth of appreciation for the skill newly won. Perhaps it comes from the swift, terrible insight that one might never be able to walk. Perhaps it comes from the desperation of facing the consequences of not walking. I am not sure of its genesis, but I observed its growth in my two young grandsons. Over the years I have felt more than once a surge of new appreciation for my legs.

There is a fierce pride in each action that makes one independent. I have often noted the contrast between my step and theirs. Although my step is not as light and easy as it once was,

I am not a prisoner to a nonfunctioning limb. During the boys' early years, I became very conscious of this ability to move around. David and Ben had to take calculated steps. They had to think about each move. They were grateful for inches. But they lost themselves in the effort, concentrating on each small movement that they could initiate and control. There was a genuine sense of achievement in what they were doing. I became more grateful and more aware and less complaining. I often recalled the line from an unidentified poet: "I had no shoes and I complained until I met a man who had no feet."

The battle these two grandsons faced was not a battle others could fight for them. Though I wanted to help, I heeded the advice I once received from a physical therapist: He told me that the worst thing anyone could do for a person struggling to make damaged muscles work was to take away the struggle. So I watched and encouraged and approved and applauded each action, but I did not lift the boys when they could lift themselves. We all knew such proffered help would be no help—worse than no help. Our help was our prayers and our encouragement.

It became abundantly clear as we had more and more individual and personal struggles to deal with that each particular disability has its own grave challenges. Defects that come at birth are like and yet unlike those that develop later, or disabling disease, or operations which become necessary.

A simple tonsillectomy no longer seems so simple when your own grandchild needs one. Amberlee had to have her tonsils out when she was just eight years old. Her mother and I sat in her hospital room before she went into surgery. She seemed calm and confident that all would go well. The hospital staff handled her case as matter-of-factly as they did those of all of the other children there. Some children came with deformities that wanted correcting. Others needed tubes in their ears. Amberlee needed a tonsillectomy to rid her body of continuing infection.

We talked together about many things that morning. I asked her about school, and she told me about her studies, about the friends she loved in her classroom, and about some of her least favorite things. She talked about her brothers and sisters—all of whom were at home eagerly awaiting her return.

She also told me about the blessing that her father had given to her before she came to the hospital. She knew there were lots of prayers being offered for her, and they put her heart at ease.

As we waited for the surgical procedure to be completed, her mother and I talked about the Lord's comment in the scripture that it was necessary for us to know both the good and the bad in order to appreciate the full growth potential of the mortal experience.

I was relieved and felt an overwhelming wave of gratitude sweep over me when Amberlee was back in her room recuperating after the surgery was all over. It was exciting to see her sitting up and talking and feeling so well. "Everything went just fine, Grandma," she said when she saw me.

The calmness of this little eight-year-old girl was amazing to me. She is a cheerful, smiling, motivated little girl who has blessed us all with her continuing happy heart, a gift from birth.

I smiled back at her and told her I had felt all along that she would be fine, but she really looked better than I had expected. She went home to Orem, and continuing telephone calls assured me that she could handle things and was looking forward to being back in school soon.

As I considered this grandchild I realized that the Lord was helping me to grow again. The words of a hymn came to mind: "More holiness give me . . . more trust in the Lord." I thought of the many times I had been at the hospital when a grandchild was born, of the many times I had given the child its first at-home bath, tended, fed, entertained the children and listened to their experiences, each one enriching my own—even in tonsillectomies. I thought, I have prayed but I have not let my soul be calm, because I have not truly accepted the peaceful calm I sought. Amberlee did.

Accidents are something entirely new again. Chance, unlooked-for injury or hurt as well as unforeseen, unexpected, and certainly undesigned accidents bring enormous stress.

Such a time came to our grandson Grant when he was only three. His mother and her sisters had taken their children to the park to play. They had barely arrived when they ran for the swings. Grant, the smallest of three brothers, took a little longer to reach the swings. As he did, he ran in front of a brother who was already swinging. Grant was knocked to the ground, his nose was caught on a protruding part of the swing, and a big piece of the flesh ripped out in a ragged tear. Everyone ran to help him, but it was obvious that he needed more assistance than his family could give him. He was rushed to the hospital. Doctors began the skilled sewing of the tear in an effort to bring back to that dear little face the form it had before the accident.

Grant had a very difficult time. He could not understand the stitches, nor the pain, nor the interruption of his play. When he came to our home there seemed to be a terrible battle within him to be freed from the pain and the bother of the bandage. His spirit was so restless that he refused to be held or comforted or calmed.

Sometimes it takes watching such a thing happen to gain a clear understanding of how important it is to control one's responses to unexpected, unwanted emergencies. None of us can control the circumstances of our lives, but in the control of our responses we gain the fullest growth—the growth which leads us closer to productive use of energy, strength, and resources.

Watching my grandson that day as he resisted the caring we offered, I gained a new insight into freedom. We all want to be free to act voluntarily without restraint by things beyond our control. Sometimes the hurt of a sudden accident so upsets our lives that we do not recover. Most often the events set in motion by the accident have a profound influence upon our lives. We must understand how to keep from being enslaved either by those things that are thrust upon us or by the actions of our own choosing. I wanted to explain this to my small grandson, but he was hurting and too young to know what I was talking about. I could not help him. He did listen to the priesthood blessing given him. During those few minutes he was quiet and calm.

Scott, another grandson, also had a terrible trauma at the age of three. His parents took him to visit his maternal grandparents at their ranch for his birthday celebration. They had all walked together as far as the barn when a sudden gust of wind whipped by, picked up a barn door that had come off, and dropped the door on Scott. He was too little to push it off. Everybody knew as they pulled the door away from that scared little boy that he was badly hurt. They rushed him to a hospital in Salt Lake City.

The doctors found that he had broken his leg and his collarbone. His parents and grandparents felt he was very fortunate that none of the long, rusty screws had hit his face or other vital parts of his body.

Everybody brought him gifts. After all, it was his birthday—and the hospital was not where he had planned to spend it. When he returned home, the pain was so intense that he had a hard time enjoying the presents.

Each day this active little boy got more and more restless, confined as he was by the cast and the hurt. Each day when we arrived to visit with him we noticed that he would not stay on the couch. He wanted to get off. He quickly found that he could. When on the floor he scooted himself around, and he could get whatever he wanted. We could not believe the creative imagination of that child in meeting the limitations of his new physical condition. He soon learned that with aspirin to dull the pain he could be up and going and happy with the challenge. We discovered that he was especially observant and vigorous and that he was capable of some very good thinking. His self-assurance at such an early age portended qualities of greatness.

His efforts gave us a deeper appreciation of something we had known for a good many years—deep within each soul there is the power and the ability to meet new circumstances with creative cheerfulness and compensation for any loss while developing new skills.

Scott was a master at all of those flexibilities.

With the birth of each grandchild, one becomes more and more aware of the value of life and of the reality that life has lights and darks. Good and bad things happen to both good and bad people. No life is free of the pain and the sorrow which comes from being mortal. Sometimes, indeed many times, our afflictions help us to seek him who has given us life. The Lord waits by the door for our knock; it is truly a blessing to realize this.

The French author Madame de Stael, writing when the world's calendar turned from the 1700s to the 1800s, observed, ''We understand death for the first time when he puts his hand upon one whom we love.''

My husband and I had known something of death before we became grandparents. We understood death a little because he had put his hand upon those we loved—our nephew, our parents, and our grandparents, as well as aunts, uncles, and cousins.

In our extended family my mother died first. I felt that my security went with her. I had always been able to call her and discuss any problem or plan, always sure that I had her full attention. We had traveled together and worked together in all of the household tasks. We had entertained and even studied together as we both served in Relief Society positions of responsibility at the same time. She was my ideal, my example, and I loved her. Suddenly she was gone. I wept and wanted to go with her. Gradually, I came to know that she did not live so that I could die when she did. Instead, she lived so that I might learn from her and teach my children and my grandchildren as she had done. Mother lived the principles of truth and righteousness as fully as she possibly could. I knew that the time would come, if I lived my life worthily as she had lived hers, that we would be together again. I was comforted.

I thought of how quickly Doug's grandfather passed away as he was working out in his garden. Doug's grandmother lived on for a few years after him but finally died, saying how much she wanted to go and be with those who had gone before her.

My grandfather died of cancer. We watched him die a bit at a time and felt he was too good a man to suffer so. And my father's passing came during the administration of a blessing in the household of faith.

Then Doug's father died of cancer of the stomach. Losing him was hard. Doug and I, even in our older years, felt like orphans. We loved our parents and wanted them to be with us always.

But none of these deaths prepared us for the death of Catherine and Carl's infant daughter. She had been born prematurely and was not able to rally. We came to understand a new dimension of death. It is one thing when death comes as a benediction to a life fully lived, but it is another when death comes just a few short days after the breath of life enters the body.

That baby was so little. She was perfect in every detail but desperately needed more months to grow and mature. The hospital staff asked, "What do you want us to do? We don't believe she has a chance of survival." There was no hesitation as her father replied, "Please do everything possible to keep her alive." They assured him they would but suggested that he and her attending physicians give her a name and a blessing. The little girl did not make it.

Catherine and Carl decided to hold only a graveside service. I did not attend. Instead I stayed with their oldest child, who had developed a serious illness and a high fever. They didn't want to leave him with anyone else. Life seemed so very fragile just then. They felt a special need to cling to their little son.

When they came back from the simple service, Catherine felt she had to go to the store. Carl stayed to be near Joshua even though the boy was sleeping. We had a chance to talk. I told him how grateful I was to see what a good father he had become. I was deeply moved by his sweet, caring manner.

Catherine had not known Carl very well nor very long when they decided to marry, and I had worried a lot about their differences. I had grown much in appreciation of him since then. Now in the quiet pause which this death had brought to both of us, I knew that this fine young man who loved my daughter and their children was a man of great tenderness.

"Carl," I said to him. "I want to apologize to you. You know that I did not feel happy about your marriage with Catherine."

"I know," he said softly. All the pretense that had grown up between us was gone at this sacred moment. His infant daughter had just been buried.

He said, "You do not owe me an apology. Rather it is I who owe you an apology. It was not until I had children of my own that I could realize how deeply a parent cares and loves and seeks to protect the children given to him or to her."

We were quiet then. Both of us knew we had experienced considerable growth. In both of our hearts there was love where it had not been, and there was understanding, also.

The death of an infant child opened our hearts to a total healing.

Seek not to counsel the Lord, but to take
counsel from him.

— Jacob 4:10

CHAPTER FIVE

Growing Through Problems

One of the challenges of being a grandmother comes in learning how to deal with the totally unexpected problems. As long as life goes along at a given pace and the problems are all anticipated, the rhythms of one's own responsibilities are uninterrupted.

But life does not always proceed as expected; then one's heart and mind must learn to handle some challenging and definite problems. In the famous lines of Edna St. Vincent Millay:

> The world stands out on either side
> No wider than the heart is wide;
> Above the world is stretched the sky, —
> No higher than the soul is high.
> The heart can push the sea and land
> Farther away on either hand;
> The soul can split the sky in two,
> And let the face of God shine through.
> But East and West will pinch the heart

> That can not keep them pushed apart;
> And he whose soul is flat — the sky
> Will cave in on him by and by.

I am not certain that the poet had in mind the problems of a heart made lonely by childlessness nor the barren spots of a heart that did not initially consider the idea of adoption as a solution to a daughter's problem. But I am sure my grandmother's heart was pushed wide open when I came to appreciate the joy of accepting into the family a new child who had not been born through my children.

Sandra, our oldest daughter, had been married about five years, and by this time medical authorities confirmed the fact that there probably would not be a natural conception.

She had taught school during these years and had come to love many other people's children. To some of the children she felt particularly drawn; to all of them she felt very close, and this seemed to add to the haunting feeling of empty arms. Some of her students she admired for all they could do. To others she gave extra effort, for she could see them just a little short of their potential. All of the children mattered to her.

She often spoke of two little black children she taught. They had been adopted by a white woman while she was touring in Africa. The children had been badly abused. The woman was so tender and loving to those little children and she cared so completely for their needs that they always came to school happy, clean, well fed, and anxious to learn. They were good students, and Sandra could see the value of a solid home life and the loving care that was necessary for physical growth and intellectual development. The other students seemed to take on Sandra's accepting and admiring attitude. Those two were the only black students in the school at that time, and an atmosphere of openness toward them was imperative for their success.

And there was Betsy, a brilliant, delightful, unassuming child. Sandra didn't really think that Betsy understood how mentally superior she was to all of her classmates. Her detailed reports were extraordinary. She could finish her assignments in just minutes and always have everything correct. In order to help her feel comfortable and stay with the class, her parents challenged her at home by teaching her interesting things like cryptology. Watching that child helped Sandra to appreciate the work of good parents.

David came to her classroom without many of the skills her other students had been taught, and Sandra spent endless hours working with him. I remember David's mother resenting the strict discipline of Sandra's class until she discovered that her son was developing life-long skills for which she knew he would be eternally grateful. Sandra was pleased and knew that she too was learning life-long skills from her classroom experience.

She waited anxiously for the day when she could try them at home. The love of children which Sandra had developed while growing up at home and during her schoolteaching years grew more and more intense. When her younger sister, Lillian, announced at a family party that she was expecting a baby, Sandra was thrilled for her—but being thrilled for someone else did not make the emptiness go away.

The childless couple had been to doctors seeking medical advice. It was a heartbroken young woman who sobbed out to me, "Oh, Mother, I want to have a baby so very much. Now, after all these years of marriage, the doctors tell us that there is almost no chance for us to have children of our own."

The desperate, disappointed cry through the telephone made me want to take her in my arms and comfort her as I had done so many times in years gone by. But I could not.

Then came to my mind a conversation of just a few days earlier about a doctor who made a particular effort to place babies in Latter-day Saint homes.

"Have you thought about adoption?" I asked.

"Not really." Her voice sounded very far away.

"How would you feel about it?" she asked me.

She wanted to know if I would be able to love an adopted grandchild as much as the one who had been born to her sister. She didn't ask me in so many words, but she wanted to know if I could and if she could. I told her I could. I was sure I could. She sighed and said that she guessed this might be the answer. She wanted to talk it over with her husband.

"I do want a baby . . . so very much," she whispered.

I said, "It seems like the very best thing to do under these conditions. I have a friend who has just had an adoption in her family. Why don't you talk to your husband and see how he feels? In the meantime I will check with my friend and find out all of the details."

The telephone conversation turned from helplessness to hopefulness.

Shortly she called again from California where they were living and said that they both agreed it would be the best thing for them to do. Her next question was, "What did you find out? To whom can I write? Can I call someone? What can I do?"

I called my brother, for whom this doctor had found a baby just months before. He called the doctor and the search was on. He talked with Sandra and had her write a short letter of request. Then came the waiting.

Sandra's grieving turned into a determined effort to do what she could to make her home a happy place for children—her own, other people's, her sister's—all children. The possibility of adoption carried with it a cautious excitement.

When Lillian announced the forthcoming birth of a second child, Sandra's intense feelings of desire to have a baby in her house increased.

It wasn't until after Christmas 1968 that Sandra and her husband returned to California to find a letter informing them that their baby would be born near the end of February. They were elated. They would have a baby of their very own before the next Christmas.

The whole family was filled with anxious expectation during those next two months. We went shopping for layette items to send down to Sandra. We wrote letters of congratulations and asked her to be sure and call us whenever she heard anything about the baby. The doctor was wonderful. He gave the parents-to-be all of the details about what the parents looked like, their background, their education—just everything. He wanted them to be completely prepared for the baby when it was born.

Finally the call came that said the baby had been born. I was happy to hear an excited voice on the other end: "Mother, we can pick up our baby girl tomorrow. She was born yesterday. Will you please fly down and be with us? It is all so new to me."

I boarded the flight early the next morning. They met me at the airport. We drove to the hospital. They went into the nursery with a brand-new gown, diapers, blanket, shirt, and shawl all freshly laundered. They came out with a wide-eyed, beautiful, three-day-old baby girl all their very own.

Sandra said with wonder, "She was wide awake, just waiting for us."

The four of us crowded into the front seat of the car so we could all see the baby. We wanted to watch her every movement on the long ride home. She continued, wide-eyed, watching us for nearly an hour, and then she fell contentedly to sleep. The nurses had said that she had been sick during those first three days and had had a difficult time tolerating anything to eat. Now she seemed at peace.

She was a perfect baby for my daughter and her husband. She adjusted almost immediately to the routine of their home, loved her bath, enjoyed the food, and ate and slept. In the beautiful nursery they had prepared for her she was at home. The orange, yellow, and green colors were cheerful, and the perky white curtains blew lightly in the breeze. That baby fit perfectly into that beautiful setting. Of course, I could love her as much as my other grandchildren. "Was it more?" I kept asking myself. I knew how desperately she was wanted, and I was filled with incomparable happiness now that she was safely in their keeping.

We all marvelled at her happy spirit. She grew by leaps and bounds day by day.

Now we had a new joy to look forward to—we could hardly wait to take her to the temple and have her sealed to us for time and all eternity. It seemed as if the day would never come.

We were constantly on our knees praying that nothing would go wrong before the day came. Because she was born in California, it took eighteen months plus a day in court to legalize and finalize the adoption.

Then, at last, we were all there around the altar in that holy house. I knew that God had given this child to my child to love and to raise. I thought about the fact that God honored adoption as a process, for he had provided that children could be adopted into the house of Israel, that we could become the adopted sons and daughters of Jesus Christ if we lived worthily.

I remember how I prayed there at that lovely moment. "Help each of us have the vision of life and its purposes. Let us dedicate ourselves to living so that we might attain the great fulfillment that is possible." There were tears of happiness from the new parents for the baby that had come to bless their home. There were tears of happiness from those of us who were grandparents, with gratitude that these two children would not miss the challenge of being parents. If only those feelings could be remembered and the living of each day could be blessed by the feeling of unity that was there with us in that holy place.

I have thought a great deal about unity. How can a large family with many different individuals come to a feeling of unity? As I entered into the role of grandmother, I was certain of one thing: I wanted unity in my family. I wanted to be helpful and useful to my children and their children. With this in mind I greeted the birth of each of my grandchildren with a burst of energetic helping. I would go to care for the home and the other children while the mother and the new baby adjusted to the complexities of adding a new person to the daily routines of each household. I could do dishes and I could fix meals and I could encourage and answer questions.

I always felt confident of my welcome into the home for these brief interludes. In between births I thought about how to be helpful and useful. I wondered what other things I might do to be a good grandmother.

In my conversations with my children I picked up a lot of clues. I found that it was better to call my children personally to deliver family messages. Sometimes when I sent word by another child there were wounded feelings and some felt less valued than others.

It had never been intended that way. Sometimes I had asked another to call just to be more efficient. Especially was this true when I was the general president of the Relief Society and I wanted everyone to come to a Sunday dinner at my house, or when I was organizing a large family activity. As soon as I learned that the practice piqued the feelings of some of my family I changed. Instead of one call I would list the name of each child and the telephone number by it; I would write the message I wanted to deliver and then make the telephone calls in between appointments. I would continue until I had a check by each name. Characteristically, I move methodically to accomplish a task once I determine what needs to be accomplished. This had been true in my school years and during my community and church service. It was also true of me as a mother.

I thought I would be a valued ally to my children, helping them in the very real, nitty-gritty, burdensome work of each day. I was never one to shy away from the hard tasks but followed the training my mother had given me. I remember well the days when she had thirty-two shirts to iron. She would get up early and begin. If she wasn't through when we children came down to breakfast, she would stop long enough to feed us; but the shirts were finished before she began on her other chores.

I never meant to take over the primary work of the family that belonged to a mother and father. I knew they had to establish the patterns of their own homes, and I knew they had to be responsible for the disciplining and training of their own children.

Nevertheless I felt perfectly comfortable going into their homes and freely pitching in. It never occurred to me not to do so. I spent many hours considering the needs of each of my children's families, and I planned ways to be responsive to those needs in between meetings, assignments, and my own home responsibilities. I wanted to be helpful. I believe the hallmark of being a good grandmother is to be useful.

In this spirit I listened one day when one of my daughters said that it was very hard to come home from a lovely trip to a messy house. Pricked by conscience (I was trying to deal with feelings that I had been negligent because of my Church responsibilities), I resolved to be responsive to what I interpreted as a plea for help.

The next time this daughter went out of town she asked someone to stay with her children. I felt anxious to be useful, and I considered what I might do. I remembered our earlier conversation, so I took a day off from my Relief Society duties and called the caretaker of the children and arranged to spend the day before they came home cleaning the house and making it shiny and orderly for the homecoming.

Bright and early I drove to my daughter's house and proceeded to pitch into the tasks of cleaning. When I was through the house looked lovely. Then I suggested that the baby tender return home, and I would take the children to my home so that their house would be clean for the returning parents.

She agreed and I went to gather the children up. Most of the children felt happy about the idea except the oldest son, a child I had felt very close to. When the idea was presented to him, he went on what seemed to me to be a rampage. He had things to do and would not hear of such a change in plans. I felt verbally abused and deeply hurt.

The day so dearly won from the multitude of responsibilities I had and the hard work I had entered into so freely, desiring only to be of service to my children and their children, was turning into a nightmare. I took some of the children with me, left him there, and returned to my home devastated.

The next day as I met my daughter and her husband, I briefly explained the fiasco of the night before. My son-in-law seemed to understand and said he would speak to his son. My daughter was troubled. I was more hurt than I had ever been before. When they returned to their home, their displeasure intensified, and my behavior was viewed so critically that I could not keep from weeping.

The work I had done with so much love was rejected. In some way I had overstepped the bounds of a grandmother. I was totally at fault in their eyes.

The results of that incident have been very difficult for me. No more the free and easy access into my children's homes and lives. No more the ready step into getting the work of the moment under way. No more the sense of unqualified welcome. Not in that home or in any of the other homes. I am now much more cautious.

I have learned that a grandmother should not go into any home in the family without an invitation. A grandmother may not assume any responsibility in a child's home that is not specifically delegated.

It has been a bitter lesson to learn, but I believe I have grown even in this uncomfortable situation. I believe there is reason to think I am increasing in wisdom. I must learn more about being counseled than giving counsel.

Without any question the most difficult of the adversities which have come to our large family of families is the divorce one of our daughters has recently experienced.

I never thought it would come to our family. We were and are committed to the principles of the gospel of Jesus Christ. We have worked hard at developing unity within our ranks. We measure our actions against the teachings we have learned throughout a lifetime.

The primary relationship between a husband and wife is beyond the reach of parent or grandparent initiative. We can only help pick up the pieces of the shattered family and offer solace to the souls of those so deeply shaken.

It is possible to see with clarity the wisdom of President Spencer W. Kimball's statement that divorce comes through selfishness and through an unwillingness to let the renewing spirit of love enter into even the most difficult of problems in order that we might receive help from the Lord.

A friend once came to me and told me of her divorce. As she did she recounted all of the good things about her husband and the four children he brought to their marriage after the mother of the children had died of cancer. As she told me about her husband and the probable reasons why after twenty years he had determined to leave her, she said, "This much I know. The Lord has given me the gift of love, and no one is going to take it from me. I will continue to love my husband and be grateful for the good days we had together. I will continue to love his children and our children and find as many ways as possible to share those feelings with them." I could not believe anyone could go through the bitterness and the anguish of divorce without letting the destructive influences of hate and hurt embitter her.

When I finished talking to her I knew more of the challenge

that was ahead for my husband and me as grandparents, as a family, and for my daughter and her children. I hope we can help them hold fast to the gift of love so that it might not be taken from their lives.

There will be more long hours of searching our souls and listening to the cries of the wounded to find the ways in which we might best offer the healing solace of understanding hearts and overcome the problems so that the nurturing of loving actions might be welcomed and freely accepted. I hope all of the members of our family will concentrate on a resolve not to let the gift of love be taken from them.

But covet earnestly the best gifts: and yet
shew I unto you a more excellent way.
— 1 Corinthians 12:31

CHAPTER SIX

Growing Into New Family Traditions

A short time ago I made a trip to California. My travels took me to see two well-known buildings, famous landmarks that made me think a great deal.

One was the Winchester Mystery House in San Jose. This rambling house was the home of Sarah L. Winchester, heiress to the Winchester Rifle fortune. She lived in the house, according to the guide, from 1884 to 1922. She believed that she would be allowed to remain alive as long as she kept building.

She had become convinced that the lives of her husband and baby daughter had been taken by the spirits of those killed by the "gun that won the West." She felt that she would be taken unless she began building a mansion for the spirits and determined that the work on the mansion would never stop.

So with one thousand dollars a day in royalties from the Winchester Rifle manufacturing companies, she ordered the work to begin. The sounds of the carpenter's work could be heard twenty-four hours a day for almost thirty-eight years as the diminutive woman built to live.

She built a house of one hundred sixty rooms with forty-seven fireplaces and ten thousand windows. She used the number thirteen in many ways: there were thirteen bathrooms and in many places thirteen windows grouped together. In one room she had a staircase built with thirteen steps that led up to the ceiling. Doors opened on to blank walls. Along with this weird construction she hired artists to give the structure great beauty of design and to buy furnishings of exquisite taste and often at great expense.

The building is still in the process of being restored to its original luster. Sons and grandsons of great artisans have been hired to help on the restoration project because the house is purported to represent a dynamic chapter in a fascinating period of American life.

The other building I visited is found in Sacramento, California. It is the magnificent state capitol building which has recently been completely restored to its original grandeur.

Now the capitol building is earthquakeproof, and inside its walls is the safe repository of much of California's rich history. The beauty of the early period is captured by the skill and the artistry of those working on the restoration. The early builders were men and women of courage, strength, accomplishment, and development. They had enthusiasm and much faith in their new state and wanted the building to reflect their vision.

In fact, those early builders wanted to have everything up-to-date in the capitol, but there were limitations to their technology. We soon found that out as we listened to the guide. He asked one of the visitors to read a telegram that was sitting on the desk of the governor. The telegram was from the president of the United States in 1906. He said that he had just heard by rumor that there had been an earthquake and a fire in California. He wired to ask the governor to confirm or deny the rumor by return telegram. We wondered why he didn't just place a telephone call. Our guide anticipated our question and with a lighthearted response said: "The telephone was only for calling people within the building and for a few who lived within a short mile radius. Telephones in that day were neither transcontinental nor worldwide."

As I thought about the beauty and strength of a government that cared about its people and went forward toward accomplishment, I remember also the fear and anxiety of Sarah Winchester. She had as much money as she could want but never had the peace and happiness to live in her mansion with confidence and love. Both places had been restored: one was a monument to stagnation and spiritualism. The other was a reminder of spiritual strength and of the unified relationships of a people and of the government in which they believed.

Often as I have found moments of contemplation during these years of being a grandmother, I have thought about my gratitude for a fundamental gospel foundation and a framework of meaning upon which to build my life and to shape the life of our family now growing more numerous and more complex each day. I am aware that our family is now a superstructure which houses seven families.

One of the great challenges that comes with this growth is to try to avoid the helter-skelter approach to life as found in the mysterious old Winchester house. It takes considerable thought and planning to come up with some shared family experiences that provide meaningful opportunities for growth for each member of the family. When we get through our family building, I trust it will look more like the state capitol than the Winchester mansion.

In the beginning I found it easy to enter into the lives of my children and grandchildren by doing the natural helpful things that give comfort, instruction, and relief to the anxious first-time mother as well as to the experienced mother who must deal with many lives in different areas of need.

As the number of grandchildren has increased, it has become a greater challenge to plan Smith family activities that have interest and meaning and that do not end in utter chaos.

At first my husband and I issued the usual invitation to all married children to come home to Sunday dinner. We continually expanded and reduced the dining room table over those first few years. Then Church assignments or illness would make it impossible for first one and then another to be with us. On other occasions they would have guests. If appropriate, those guests might be included too. We never really knew until the very hour how many or how few might sit down to eat dinner with us on a given Sunday.

The dinner conversation changed over the years, too. One Sunday the children excused themselves one by one and began playing with their cousins while their parents engaged in reminiscing. Then we heard peals of laughter. One blonde, blue-eyed child appeared with Magic Marker all over her face. Her mother didn't think it was at all funny. Panic-stricken, she thought that she might also have written on the furniture. She had. It was a leather chair. Her mother had removed Magic Marker before by spraying it with hair spray, and fortunately it worked. The children were given strict orders to put the Magic Markers away, and the mother again joined in the discussions that were still going on around the table.

Soon we heard a scream and a little boy came out with a bloody nose. He was surrounded by concerned little girls. "He wanted to play house with us and we didn't want him to, so we put this pan on his head. We must have hit his nose." It was another child but the same mother. Embarrassed, she quickly took all of her children and left.

I knew the children could not be blamed. As adults we were just enjoying ourselves and not even trying to direct the little ones. I thought about the problem and decided that I should follow the pattern carried out in Relief Society. They didn't expect the children to entertain themselves unsupervised, and neither must we. After that, whenever we were together, we planned things for the children to do, things for the adults to do, and things for adults and children to do together. It took some good organization but it has worked well for us.

As the years went on, it became more difficult for me to cook dinner for the whole family (now numbering forty-eight) once a week. The girls were very thoughtful and helpful; still it was a big job. In addition, the Sunday meeting schedule and ward and stake responsibilities of each family made it almost impossible to continue having Sunday dinner on a weekly basis. We were determined that we would still have family gatherings but not necessarily on Sunday. We all began looking for just the right activity.

One idea came while I was serving as the general president of the Relief Society. I was invited to attend the Manti pageant and to bring my family. I had already been to that spectacular religious production held on the temple grounds in Manti, Utah. It occurred to me that my family had not seen it and that since it was held outdoors my large family would not be a problem, so I picked up the telephone, called, and asked if the invitation really could be extended to my children and grandchildren. I was assured it would be not only fine but appreciated, too. I then called each family and asked if they would like me to accept the invitation in their behalf. There was a very receptive spirit.

My husband and I decided that we should all go on a bus together; in that way we could all ride and visit while going down to the pageant and coming home.

I put up lunches in some charming lunchboxes, one for each person. I then assigned one adult or one older grandchild to each little child as a partner. It was the partner's responsibility to see that his or her assigned child had sufficient to eat, that he could play the games we organized for the bus trip to Manti, that the child was able to see the pageant, that he was warm and comfortable, and that he got back on the bus after the pageant.

After everyone had been assigned a partner and the lunchboxes were passed out, we were waiting for the bus when I saw one little three-year-old boy with two boxes. I turned to my great big husky son and asked, "Isn't he your partner?"

"Yes, he is!" came the immediate reply.

"Then why is he carrying two lunchboxes?" I questioned.

"Because he is my partner and he is supposed to help me," my son smiled with his answer. That little boy was just as proud as he could be when he told me he was carrying lunch for his "partner."

Some of the children had never ridden on a bus before and were excited to get on. We had lots of fun on the bus. One adult told the story of the pioneers. Another led us in singing songs. Another had travel games for us to play. I believe the most fun was when a dear friend taught us how to play regular tablespoons and make the rhythm of music. We played our spoons right up to our arrival at the Manti pageant grounds. We were about the last busload of people to arrive so we hurried right in, sat down, and the pageant began. It was a wonderful night and a splendid performance. Since we were the last ones getting there we were also the first ones out. Nearly everyone slept on the bus going home.

Encouraged by the success of this pleasant large gathering of the Douglas Smith clan, I began to feel the desirability of an annual family summer activity with our children and our grandchildren.

I invited a representative from each family. We all met and decided to go to Midway, Utah, for a three-day outing the next summer. We began with a road rally to get us there. We were clocked as we began, and we had very specific road signs to note and speed checks to consider as we traveled. We had car activities as part of the rally. The route was identified in rhyme, as we wanted to really challenge each carload of family members. Each car was checked in as it crossed the last road marker, and the driver handed the checker his starting time. When it was computed, we had the trophy-winning car of the road rally and were on our way to a fun-filled holiday.

Each family was given a menu of activities and asked to check the ones in which they wanted to participate. Most of them came back with everything marked. We had swimming, golfing, fishing, horseback riding, bicycling, shuffleboard, and table tennis. We had coloring contests, storytelling time, balloon soccer, Old Maid, Go Fishing, and Rook. We knew everyone wanted to eat around a bonfire and sing, so that had also been arranged. Every minute of the day could be filled with active participation or there could be quiet time. One thing we were was flexible.

Our large family outings are of recent origin, and we are still diversifying. Sometimes current events shape our plans. The year the United States hosted the summer Olympics in Los Angeles, all eyes were upon the excitement of that great competition. We decided to hold our own Smith family summer Olympics. Again we chose to go to Midway.

As before, we began with a family representative meeting in committee. Each one was to go home and talk with the family and see what kinds of competition they would enjoy. Then we were to meet and see that something was planned for each member of the family from the littlest baby to the oldest adults . . . the grandparents. We made "observer" as well as "participant" badges and gave medals for both. After all, what fun is competition if there is no one there to cheer you on?

We began with a grand entrée. The families marched onto our arena with family banners held high. There was a torch lighting ceremony and family song. After all contestants were told of the events and the rules for winning the medals, we began.

We had bottle-drinking contests for the babies and crawling contests for those too little to walk. We had butterfly-catching contests for the two-year-olds, with butterfly nets of netting and reshaped metal coat hangers. You should have seen the toddlers go after the paper butterflies that were placed on the shrubbery.

Our equestrian ride was marked by a string around a pond, up a little hill, past a pine tree, and back to the beginning. The horse was a hobby horse. Those children rode for their lives as if nothing else mattered, perhaps because of that wonderful cheering section all around the marked course. The surprising thing to me was that not only the three- and four-year-olds wanted to ride, but also those six and seven and then eight and nine — and, finally, even our teenagers were good enough sports to say, "Let me try too." This increased the fun.

The swimming contest was the most professional part of our Olympics because some of our family members are swimmers who have participated successfully in swim meets. We all watched and shouted for them at the top of our lungs.

It was hard to see each day end. We just wanted it to continue on and on. But when the darkness of night took over, each little child and the parents made their way to a room marked with the Olympic symbol and their name on the door. When it closed the family knew more about excellence in performance, more about personal discipline, more about caring. Sarah tumbled into bed almost exhausted and began to dream. Her parents had just dozed off when they heard her yell, "You can do it, Steven, you can do it!" and they rested knowing that she had learned more about love that day. Our activity had succeeded. We shared some time and made new memories.

None of our activities has been more satisfying than our annual family conference. It isn't just a family home evening. For a four-hour period we try to follow the pattern of a ward, stake, or general conference. We assign a theme and speakers. As family patriarch, my husband presides over and conducts the meeting planned and carried out under his direction. We don't want it to be a babytending experience, so only those over twelve years of age are invited. After an opening session, we hold a priesthood and a Relief Society session and then a concluding session. We eat dinner together, the grandchildren serving their parents so that they can learn to give of themselves to them.

We have youth speakers and panel discussions. We try to follow the counsel of the Brethren as given at conference time to see how fully we can make application of their words in our family situation. It is a very satisfying experience to listen to our children expound the gospel of Jesus Christ and to use as examples in their talks the lives of the grandchildren whom we know and love.

It isn't easy to give serious messages to those who know us so well, and yet no group listens more empathetically and responds more fully than the family.

When our first grandchild entered the mission field we decided to resurrect an old family tradition. When each of our sons, Barton, Lowell, and Blaine, had gone on missions, I decided that they would like to hear from all of the members of the family, not just from their father and mother. This led to the establishment of the Smith Family Newsletter, which was published weekly. I asked everyone to submit a column, and then I had it put together and run off. We would sometimes glue a picture onto the lead story sheet. It was a rewarding and wonderful way to keep everyone current on family activities and events. It wasn't hard; it just took a lot of time to get the articles in to the editor.

One son saved every copy and noted that together they actually contained a brief but combined history of our family during that period. It was discontinued when all of the boys were home again from their missionary labors and when Lillian and Claron came home after his medical training was completed.

This year when young Claron Douglas went into the mission field, I decided the publication should resume. Everybody agreed. We hope to accomplish four major purposes with our newsletter:

1. To keep our missionary informed regarding family activities.
2. To give our missionary an opportunity to write one letter each month to the whole family and in this way save him time from sending individualized letters to each family.
3. To be a wonderful teaching tool to the other grandchildren and help them to learn the importance of missionary work.
4. To be a brief history of the family at this time of our lives.

It has been again a time-consuming experience, although different because I now have a computer to help me. I can call and get articles from each family and type them into the computer.

When it comes to assembling the paper, we use a newsroom layout program. Our son Barton comes up, often with his family, and does the graphics, and we work together until it is published. Doug runs it off and mails it out.

We are watching the paper grow. I have been interested to see that some of the young children want to add a column of their own. The children and the grandchildren seem to be very interested and want to be part of this activity. It is also a good way to notify the family of upcoming events and make certain the information is accurately passed on to all of the members of the family.

One of the challenges of a large family is keeping everyone informed of each other's activities, and in this regard our newspaper has served us well.

The newspaper has become a Smith family tradition.

Traveling together is another tradition born anew in the generation which has followed me. The fun of a shared trip makes memories which enrich and enliven in all the years which follow it for all who participate.

I think that is why our granddaughter Allison did not want to miss the family trip this summer even though she was quite ill. Sometimes she had to stay in the hotel room because she was not able to keep up with her sisters and little brother. But she was there and she shared in the visits to Church historical sites. More than that, she shared in the fun and the comradery.

Everybody has different traditions.

Families need to develop new traditions through the years as circumstances change and grandchildren come.

Tradition—as the fiddler on the roof in the musical of the same name explains—is what binds us together and keeps us moving and feeling and behaving in time-honored ways. Many times, as the Jewish people have found, it is tradition which preserves life and values when all else seems to conspire to destroy.

A wise son heareth his father's
instruction.

—Proverbs 13:1

Growing Through Strengthening Family Ties

As grandparents we had to learn that we still had responsibilities as parents to our own children and to their partners
who have become our much loved children.

Therefore, we regularly get the adults of the family together
for special activities: birthday celebrations, Father's Day,
Mother's Day, holidays, reunions—for almost any occasion.
This year we really went all out: Our children and their com-
panions went to Hawaii with us, without our grandchildren. Oh,
yes, one grandchild did come—it was Sherilynn's new baby.

We had talked about it, planned, saved, and looked forward
to this vacation together for three years. I can never remember
seeing the children so excited. We held planning parties, pre-
Hawaii parties, and received almost daily reports on how all of
the arrangements were working out. Leaving thirty-four grandchildren home meant the involvement of a lot of people.

Doug and I went over to the islands early to attend a business
convention. Afterwards, we were waiting at the gate as the children arrived at the airport. Doug would not let all fourteen of

them fly on the same airplane; his concern was for the thirty-five orphans if anything should happen to the flight. I was so filled with eager anticipation that I had had a restless night. Waiting to greet them in that new place gave me a glimpse of what it might be like to be awaiting our time together as an eternal family, but I quickly put those thoughts from my mind and welcomed each one with a lei and a kiss.

We immediately went over to the interisland terminal and caught our two flights for Kauai. There rented cars were waiting for our drive to Princeville—caravan style.

Two couples had been assigned to each condominium. Of course, we had the parents of the baby and the baby in our condominium; the others were vacationing from their children, but not us. Having the baby there with us made our time on the islands more enjoyable. Everyone settled in and tried to rest for the next day.

Despite the time change everyone was up early the next morning. We quickly gathered suntan lotion, beach towels, body-surfing boards, and grass mats and were off to the beach —again caravan style. Two of our sons-in-law were very familiar with the beaches and took us to a nearly private place. There we began to have fun.

I had never really been in the ocean, so I decided I must at least do a little wading. My son took my hand and said, "Come and ride on the boogie board. You'll like it; it's great." I protested in vain. He helped me learn how to ride the waves of the ocean, and it was wonderful. The girls thought, "If Mother can do it, anyone can." Before we knew it all of us were playing in the ocean. Some were diving into the waters. All of us were enjoying ourselves. The caution given by their father in another day was not needed now because the children were older and wiser and had learned many of the lessons of safety and pleasure. The interesting thing to me was that though we were together, each one had a different determination of what he or she wanted to do and how to pass the days of happiness so long looked forward to.

The first big event the children had planned was a birthday party for their father. We had been in Hawaii on the date of his birthday, so they held a late party to honor him. Each one had written a special tribute to him and placed it in a book. They gave it to him with a kikui nut lei—a symbol of honor and respect—and then took him to a very special restaurant for dinner. Appropriately, the local people held a torch-lighting ceremony just as they had done long years ago. They were sharing their traditions with us, and we were enjoying the tradition of our many years of celebrating birthdays together.

Every day was different. Most days Blaine went out to run between four and ten miles before anyone else was up except the birds and the baby. Some members of the family slept in late; others walked over to our condominium to see what the plans were for the day. We ate breakfast and chatted about our activities. The weather was perfect and seemed to invite us to explore every part of that beautiful island.

As we talked together we took time to pick up shells. We could not believe the variety as we gathered some to take home to the grandchildren. The flowers were blooming in great profusion. We weren't able to identify as many as we wanted to, so Sherilynn bought a book that we kept close at hand to help us learn more about each flowering tree, bush, or plant. We enjoyed their fragrance as well as their beauty. Surrounded by so much loveliness, our souls felt refreshed as our minds and bodies were rejuvenated.

There was a feeling of being alone in a new world of beauty, and it seemed to me that we all were fairly drinking in the wonders of creation but were never filled.

We hated to leave that bit of heaven but were introduced to another new world when we went back to Honolulu. We had dinner with some Hawaiian and Chinese friends. They fed us delicious food. They danced and sang for us and taught us some very simple songs we could take back home. Their presentation of flowers and food and family togetherness is a treasured memory.

Some Church friends had a dinner for us on the beach of Waikiki. They too were wonderful. They brought food supreme and entertainment *par excellence*. We basked in the splendor of a Hawaiian sunset we will always remember.

We were able to come together and have such a wonderful time because we had built over many years and with special activities of the past the family ties that made possible the caring and sharing of these few days. There was the freedom to be oneself and to be respected for it. There was much talk about the grandchildren left at home, even frequent telephone calls to make certain all was well. And when their arms felt too empty they would pick up Sherilynn and Hector's baby and love her. She was delighted, even at three months, to have the attention of so many loving people. We all watched her grow and do such cute things during those days we spent with her and each other.

Many other people have found that they can build family ties by developing special activities. I have been amazed at the creativity and the love with which grandmothers throughout the Church have worked to develop close family ties. I am convinced that energy spent in such development is very valuable. For me there is nothing more rewarding than to feel the continued development of good feelings between my children and my grandchildren. I believe it will be a source of comfort, solace, strength, and faith to each of them. I know it is to Doug and to me.

One thing has become abundantly clear to me in my nineteen years as a grandmother. There is no single right way to be a grandmother. There is an infinite number of right ways. A while ago I was amused to hear from a sister in Jackson, Mississippi, that her granddaughter had asked her one day, "Grandmother, why are you so fat and my other grandmother so thin?" That delightful grandmother was a woman of great talent that she used for those grandchildren's benefit. With her charming Southern drawl she explained, "Why, child, didn't you know that grandmothers are supposed to be fat? I'm so sorry about your other grandmother being thin. Whatever do you suppose is wrong with her?"

She was taken aback a little, however, when the other grandmother called the next day and told her how quickly that conversation had come around to her with the counsel from the granddaughter that she had better put on a little weight.

This dear sister, skilled in interior design, has prepared a dolls' room in her house. It is the favorite place for the children to be. There, a charming four-poster bed and pictures take you back into another time and place. It is delightful for anyone to step into. The table and chairs invite a tea party, and dolls keep the children company on the bed and in each chair, just waiting for little girls to love them.

This tradition must have begun years before in the great-grandmother's home. It featured two beautiful little trees decorated for Easter when I visited there. She had tied plastic Easter eggs on the trees with yellow, blue, purple, and pink ribbons and two Easter bunnies with baskets at the base of the trees. She told me that just before Easter she would have the children come over and get the baskets for an Easter egg hunt. After their baskets were full, they would take them in the house with her and eat their candy eggs while she told them the story of the Resurrection.

Another acquaintance spends much time and thought on her grandchildren, too. She paints lovely flowers for them. Once she purchased some heart-shaped wooden boxes, tole-painted a different flower for each of her seven granddaughters, lined the boxes, and filled them with jewelry. She gave each girl a box with one of her personally penned notes of love, like this one:

Dearest Maria Lana,

I must have known you before you were born. How else could I feel so tenderly about you from the moment I first saw you? You have all the lovely character traits, tenderness, sensitiveness, perception, consideration that comprise the ideal girl. Because you were permitted to come to this earth at this glorious time, you were given important assignments, so I know you will succeed.

Love, Nana

One day while she was telling her little granddaughter about her plans, the little girl put her arms around her neck, loved her, kissed her, took her grandmother's hands in hers, and said, "Oh, Nana dear, I love you and your little old-fashioned hands."

Grandmothers don't all come in the same sized packages, and they don't all have the same interests. I am convinced, as I am sure each person who thinks about it must be, that being a successful grandmother is a lot like being a successful mother. There must be a great deal of love and concern and a very active desire to let that love be felt.

A good friend of mine turned her attic into a grandchildren's playroom. The stairway leading up to it was immediately off the kitchen. She could listen to them play, and she knew they liked the privacy and yet the nearness of it. She filled the room with the things she thought they would like and would develop a child's creative mind and stimulate wonderful relationships with those at Grandma's house. She put in the room a xylophone that she had played long before. She found a desk with an inscription from which she got her daughter Julie's name. Her grandchildren loved to be in that warm, close environment of the past, present, and future.

In Cedar City, Utah, I met a sister at a Relief Society function who so far has added three wonderful regular events to her life to enrich her experiences with her children and her grandchildren.

Each week she has Sunday dinner at Grandma's house. Each family comes once a month on a different week. The grandchildren continually ask, "Whose week is this week for Sunday dinner?"

Once a month she has all her grandchildren come for either a sleep-over or for a campout. While the girls are there they do things the girls want to do with their grandparents. For the boys it is other choices. The activities change from month to month, but they always have a wonderful time together.

And once every other year this grandmother plans a week at the beach in California for all of her children and grandchildren. They enjoy the beach, visit Disneyland and the San Diego Zoo, and play at things both the children and the adults can do and enjoy together.

Another time I was told about a couple who retired to Provo from California. When friends visited them, they found him building what he called his "dream" homes. He was building houses and then selling them. The grandmother had encouraged her husband to buy some property with some buildings on it. He did, and she seemed to be stuck out on that property with funny old run-down shacks. They called it their "ranch."

They began inviting their grandchildren to come and visit them and to help them turn those tumble-down buildings into places where the grandchildren could sleep and play and have fun. After they got the project of repair far enough along, they began to have "cousins' week." During this week all the cousins would come and be together at Grandma's ranch. Then the parents could travel or stay home alone or do whatever they wanted, but the cousins could be together and have fun with Grandma and Grandpa.

Over and over again the question that came to them was, "Why are you working so hard now that you are retired?" And the grandpa answered: "I've always wanted to be a contractor and build my dream home. I can't afford to keep it, so I sell it and find that my dream homes are dream homes for other people as well as for me. I'm doing exactly what I want to do." Grandma responds: "I've always wanted a place to love and to be with my grandchildren. I want them to feel free to run and play and yet feel that they are part of what is happening." So they come and help her build the ranch. The ranch is the place where the children want to be. It is, they say, "the most wonderful place in all the world."

It won't be many years before a friend will retire from the BYU continuing education program in California. When I asked him what he wanted to do when his life's work comes to an end, he said, "Perhaps I should plan some trips with my grandchildren; I've been doing that for other people for a very long time." He recounted one experience of a trip he had taken with his family and told of the planning that had gone into it. The children had been brought together in the initial planning. They determined that they needed a financial advisor, a log keeper, a social director, a nutritionist, a navigator, a cook, and a cook's helper. The children studied maps and tour books and determined educational experiences they could have as they went to different places on that trip. For example, they wanted to locate places for treasure hunts and a field where they could play ball for an hour. Each member of the family was to help instruct the others in the responsibility for every activity and the scope of individual involvement. When it was over some said of future vacations, "Is this another of Mother's field trips?" Others said they had never had such an enjoyable time nor learned so much while traveling. They laughed when they thought of one of the littlest boys who looked at the Grand Canyon for a moment and said, "Well, we've seen it, so let's go on to Fool's Creek."

Talking with a father of fifteen children, I was interested in his conclusion that families needed to spend their resources in sharing with each other. He said they always had "brag time" during their family home evenings so that each child could tell the rest of the family what he or she had accomplished. I believe one of the most significant things a grandmother can do is to be a listener for a grandchild's "brag time," whether in a group setting or in the privacy of a one-on-one experience together.

My children had a grandmother who did for them an extraordinary thing—she brought them the gift of enthusiasm. She was an adventurer. Every day, every trip, every experience was meaningful, whether with her family to Fish Lake, with the company executives to Alaska, or to the Waldorf Astoria in New York City. She was enthusiastic about everything. No one could have been a greater fan of ball games or a more competitive participant in golf, swimming, bowling, or a Rook game. No one was more appreciative as a spectator at ball games watching her sons or grandsons or while rooting for her favorite team. No one found more pleasure in delving through historical data in the research of genealogy.

My mother created a place of love for our children. They loved to "stay over" at her home. They loved singing around the piano with her. She played by ear and could accompany them as they sang any song. She would also help them if they wanted to learn how to play the piano. She read stories to them as long as they wanted to listen or as long as they could keep their eyes open. Bedtime was being tucked into crisp, clean white sheets freshly laundered and brought in from the outdoor clothesline. Sleep always came quickly, and so did morning. Breakfast was always hot cooked mush, eggs, bacon, and toast with orange marmalade. She served them fruit. It was their choice. Was it that Grandma's cooking was better than home cooking or that her loving service made these moments so memorable? Whatever it was, Grandma Bradshaw put together lots of memories for her grandchildren. The nostalgic feelings of going to Grandma's house tug and pull at the heartstrings of the children and bring her ever close even now.

Performing in public was another thing Grandma Bradshaw introduced to our children. She loved dramatics and was frequently involved in putting on plays and roadshows in the wards in which she lived. She wanted each of her grandchildren to feel like a star. She would practice with them individually and then at the next opportunity at a family gathering she would have that child perform so that we might all applaud. The happy applause was satisfying for the child and encouraged even more dedication from each grandchild. Grandma Bradshaw never developed a concert pianist or an opera singer, but there were some very good performers. At her funeral her granddaughters sang "I Think When I Read That Sweet Story of Old," and the boys were represented by Roddie, who sang "I Wonder When He Comes Again." Someone called them angels. To us they were Grandma's "stars."

Some time ago I came to know a wonderful musician, who told me that she learned to love music from her grandmother. As a child she used to go to her grandmother's home and listen through the cracks of the door to her grandmother's piano students. She said her father bought her a tennis racket hoping she would play tennis instead of the piano, but she went to a music store and said, "I've come to work for you." They thought she might be a novelty, so they hired her. She was there doing the things that would let her be close to the music that her grandmother had taught her to love. Then when Kathleen played at a Relief Society social her selection had the forty-sixth Psalm as its text. The message of the music was "be still and know that I am God." That refrain introduced at the beginning of her rendition was repeated in the middle and again in the end, and it continued to reverberate in our hearts long after she had finished playing for us. Kathleen played so beautifully that we were all touched by the music and were grateful that her grandmother had given her the desire to develop her God-given gift.

A love for music is one of many legacies that grandmothers can leave with their grandchildren. A sister from Boulder,

Colorado, told me that her grandmother did a lot of quilting. The granddaughter's job was to help her grandmother sort the pieces for the quilts. Tucked right in with the memories of the quilts and the sorting of the quilt pieces and the talking with her grandmother as she helped were the memories of her grandmother's homemade bread and potato soup. Everything was made from scratch; it was the most delicious food she had ever eaten. She remembered that because her grandfather had to have his food unsalted her grandmother would have them butter their bread and take the salt shaker and sprinkle it on the bread. "Delicious," she said.

The grandmother lived to be eighty-one years old. A widow her last twenty years, she had reared eight children. One, a little boy, died two days after a horse kicked him. Her grandmother used to exhibit her quilts at Peach Days, but she didn't enter them into the Peach Days competition, at least not in her later years. That was because she had won so many prizes that no one else felt they could win and they became discouraged. They didn't want to enter the competition any more. At that point the committee asked her to show her beautiful quilts but please not to enter the competition.

This special sister from Boulder, not yet a grandmother, is making plans for what to do when she becomes one. She will find ways to be there in times of trial, she says, and will take moments for one-on-one times with her grandchildren. Besides that she wants to have 'cousins' time,' as her friend's grandmother does; the boys can go camping with Grandfather and the girls can visit an art gallery or go to a movie or to lunch—or whatever else they want to do.

She has also determined to have a grandmother's closet. Her mother had one for her children. She put very different things in it each time they came. She remembers particularly the thread cones the children loved to play with. When her grandmother died and the funeral was held, she saw other children playing with the thread cones and had some very jealous feelings. She simply could not believe that anyone else had the right to her closet or to the thread cones . . . only the grandchildren.

Sometimes the grandmothers I have met tell me about gifts that came to them from their grandmothers unlike vacations or sleep-overs or cousins' week, but they were on-going gifts of a grandmother's talent. A certain sister shared with me that her grandmother had a most beautiful speaking voice. She read stories to her grandchildren. The stories were simply wonderful, and even though she had heard them before, they were read with such expression that she is still enriched by them. Now she tries to give that same gift to her own grandchildren, so she reads them stories and hopes to give them priceless memories in that same way.

It is the smell of gingerbread that another woman remembers from her grandmother's house. Another grandmother quoted her grandson who said, "I must be the very strongest boy in the whole world!" When his grandmother questioned him, he said: "It's all that good food you give me. Look, this meat is for my bones, this milk is for my teeth." He went on and named all of the things his grandmother had told him. She said, "I do believe in good nutrition and I really was telling him of all the wonderful things food could do. When that little fellow began his recital of the effects of nutrition, I felt all of my efforts were worthwhile."

Other grandmothers do some exciting things by long distance. They send valentines with notes of love tucked in. They send ties for shoes so that the grandchild can remember Grandmother when she looks at those ties. They can make telephone calls on special occasions or frequently just to talk to each grandchild.

One grandmother told me that she makes three-day trips at least once a year to spend time with her grandchildren. Grandmothers can attend special events like baptisms and blessings. The grandmother who did this said she has become the favorite speaker at the baptismal service of her grandchildren.

Another grandmother has decided that she will fly to the home of each child during the year and give the parents a weekend off. She will go early enough to visit with her children and learn how the household is managed. Understanding the schedule and routine, she will plan to do things with the children that will help them know of her love.

"A grandmother's home is a place to come to, not for instruction, not for direction, not for accepting alone, but for love—just to be loved,'' said a very special grandmother I know. The infinite variety of personal needs and individual talents offers us a kaleidoscope of exquisite variation from which to choose what special activities we will develop to share with our grandchildren.

It is my hope that when we are through it will be for us as it was for a friend of mine. One of their three-year-old grandchildren was looking through the family album. Every time he saw a picture of his grandmother he put his finger on her picture and said, "Mine." She had been in the delivery room, carried him down to the nursery, and spent his first hours in mortality there with him. She felt the handling of the book and the expression "mine" were a direct result of the bonding she had with him.

That's what good activities help supply—time for bonding between the grandmother and the grandchild.

Let us therefore follow after the things
which make for peace, and things
wherewith one may edify another.
                    —Romans 14:19

CHAPTER EIGHT

Growing Through Enrichment

After a grandmother has learned some fundamental ways to be useful, there comes the joy of providing enrichment in the lives of her grandchildren. Because of the rich diversity of personalities to be found among her children and her children's children, she finds the associations to be full of many-faceted challenges.

Never is life more like a textured mosaic than when one is fruitfully engaged in bringing enrichment to the lives of one's grandchildren.

During my period of service in the general presidency of the Relief Society, my assignments took me far and wide around the globe. Each time I went to another country, I tried to bring something home to my family to edify and to enrich their lives by sharing that which I had experienced and learned.

In Korea I had many experiences I wanted to share. I knew my family would be as fascinated as I was by what I saw in the homes I visited. They lived in a style very different from that my grandchildren knew. In these homes the first son was spokesman for other sons, the parents included the children in most of their activities, and the gospel was welcomed and lived as fully as those new members knew how to put it into practice. I wanted my family to hear of these exemplary Saints.

In addition, I determined to take home to each member of my family a warm parka. At this time there were twenty-six grandchildren, seven children and seven partners, and one husband. I was sure I would have trouble with customs agents who might think I meant to go into the clothing business for myself. I didn't want that hassle. Sizing and checking against the list to be certain that no one was missed or that no one lacked the appropriate size had been enough of a problem. Sure enough, as I went through the process of declaring my forty-one pieces of clothing, I could see the questions coming into the eyes of the customs agent.

Then I had an idea. I took out of my wallet a picture of all my family and tried to explain to him that these jackets were for them. He didn't understand a word I spoke, but he did understand the picture and smilingly waved me through the portals.

Most often the sharing of my visits takes an educational tack. So it was no surprise to the children and grandchildren when I invited them over and talked about my Korean adventure before bringing out the two big, new suitcases. As I opened them, out popped the coats that had been stuffed vigorously into them. It was almost like another Christmas Eve with the excitement and the passing out of those gifts.

After returning from Israel, I invited all my children to dinner and fixed foods indigenous to that nation. Then we talked about the things I had seen and the people I had met. Gale T. Boyd had been at the Church center there. She shared with me a book of her poetry. She had even enclosed some of the flowers of the Holy Land in it. I had the children listen as I read some of her lines that captured so well my feelings:

Jerusalem Night

The shadow lengthens,
it flees the falling shroud
as fire from

a dying sun
ignites the evening clouds.

The city glistens amber . . .
then as the twilight cools,
the softer light
of stars and moon
flows and glows in pools.

Cobblestones, the walls, the dome,
reflect the liquid light
as Jerusalem
of gold
turns silver in the night.

Fragrances still linger
in streets and alleyways —
from spice and incense
shuttered
in cluttered shop displays.

And blooms in terraced gardens
scent the dewy breeze
that curls about
the branches
of somber olive trees.

Relish each exotic smell,
savor every sight.
encircle them with memory,
this . . . Jerusalem night.

(From *Where David Danced*, copyright 1985 by Gale T. Boyd.
Used with permission.)

My family knew of the strife and turmoil taking place in
Jerusalem; I wanted them to feel of its beauty and industry.
And I believe they felt it as I shared my experiences and had
them eat on plates carried back from that city the same kinds of
food we ate in Jerusalem. Then we entered into a discussion
of the times of Jesus of Nazareth. Each one was given a book to
take home and read to the children so that we all might know
more of him.

"If wrinkles must be written upon our brows, let them not be written upon the heart," wrote James Abram Garfield. "The spirit should not grow old." Nothing seems more true to me. Especially was I convinced my spirit was very young and excited when I was invited in June of 1983 to see the space shuttle launched with Sally Ride aboard, the first woman astronaut to go into space. I took the VIP tour twice because there was so much to hear in order to bring back to my grandchildren the details of the space shuttle and its flight. I don't suppose the details mattered as much as the feelings I had when I watched the countdown and saw that beautiful shuttle blast off, the two hundred thousand gallons of water pour onto the launch pad, and the steam cloud up. I gathered all of the memorabilia I could to be ready for a time with my grandchildren. A former photographer for the space program gave me a model space shuttle and a patch from that flight. As I waited for the return of the shuttle, I went from one wonderful experience in Florida to another. There was so much to tell when I returned that I hardly knew where to begin.

The enrichment was doubly mine as I lived through the experiences of those days and again as I was able to share them over and over. Each grandchild was interested in a different aspect of my trip. And it was fun to share the experience one-on-one with my grandchildren, who are the inheritors of a space-linked world.

A dear friend has found that she can share her growing-up experiences. This gives the grandchildren a glimpse of another time period and a unique way of living different from that which her grandchildren know.

Sometimes Miriam talks with her grandchildren about books and articles she has read. This encourages them to read books, too, so they can talk about their findings.

She finds time to take her grandchildren on trips. Travel is unique as an enrichment of one's life, either young or old. The grandmother-grandchild combination is a great way to extend the enrichment in two directions: Grandchildren give back to grandparents a new view of everything—a view filled with excitement and wonder and the vision of youth. That makes the capturing of a shared moment especially delightful. But it also awakens in the grandmother that dormant sense of wonder and makes a trip a great adventure.

To the grandchild the grandmother offers an opportunity for a new experience and a wise and steady hand of guidance. A grandmother's interest can introduce the child to new vistas and awaken new feelings. Bringing their own insights, a grandchild and a grandmother can offer sustenance to each other along the unique path which leads to discovery.

I would probably not have been prepared to bring back the gifts and experiences of each trip if my mother-in-law had not been so thoughtful. She shared the wonders of her trips with me and with my children. We could hardly wait for her to come home. She sent postcards all along the way and then returned home with those things indigenous to the area. She looked forward to each journey as an opportunity to edify our lives as well as her own.

She did it, too, as other grandmothers do who have a talent or a handicraft that they can teach to grandchildren. She could crochet, sew, and knit, although she wasn't skilled with tools and mechanical repairs, as are some grandmothers I know.

My mother-in-law found out very early in life that sharing one's talents is not a one-way street. She prepared me for Brian, a grandchild who almost from the day of his birth gave so openly of his love that his parents, grandparents, and brothers and sisters experienced and continued to know a new dimension of love.

Brian was a wonderful baby. He almost never even whimpered. If he did, you knew something was really wrong. One wondered if he was well. He would wake up and wait patiently to be held or fed or cared for. The family thought there was a calamity if he cried. As he grew he had a great desire to go to the ranch of his maternal grandparents, to be there with the animals, with the people, and to enjoy all that these far reaches of his young life offered. The remarkable thing that he offered to his grandparents was acceptance and love. He wanted to go with his grandparents and stay with them. When any of the family would go to visit he would take hold of a hand and want us to take him in the car. There was a wonderful feeling of love because Brian was so open and loving and giving of his little self.

Some grandchildren build barriers and are reluctant to participate with grandparents. But not Brian. He wanted to go everywhere and to do everything. His open-hearted, loving way made it easy to want to share with him many things. It brought a great enrichment to the lives of those of us who were his grandparents.

A grandmother can be a special blessing to two-year-olds with a new baby in the family. Although a baby one day, the two-year-old is expected to grow up as soon as the infant is born. For some it is more difficult than for others, but for all it is a time of adjustment and accommodation. It was a very hard experience for Jason. He had been a very quiet, contented baby. He loved to be held and cuddled, but suddenly someone else was in his mother's arms and he couldn't quite understand what had happened.

He had learned to climb out of his crib and so was given a big bed of his own without restraints. He would not stay in bed. He had grown strong enough that he could and would push things over in his effort to have the time and attention that he had previously known. He was up at 2:00 or 3:00 A.M. Sometimes he stayed in bed until 4:00 A.M. and then wanted to watch television. When his parents decided that there would be no television at that time of the morning, he would fly into a tantrum. He was unable to express in words the feelings that he was experiencing. Life was difficult for Jason and for his parents as well.

How can a grandmother help bring a child from such turmoil to contentment? He knew so little of life. He had known such great love but could only feel that he had been replaced. Perhaps the responsibility and the job of being a close-at-hand grandmother in such a situation is to be able to take that child and give him the individual loving attention that a busy mother of a newborn cannot give at that moment. Perhaps in a shower of attention, it may be possible to calm his troubled heart and reassure him of his important place in the family until he gets acquainted with the new child and feels the outpouring of love the baby brings to the family. Soft, quiet words might help him learn to express himself confidently, to understand more of his vital place in the family life that has changed so quickly and so completely from his point of view.

"Mother, I really need help with Jason today," Sherilynn said as I was on my way out to the airport to meet a friend. "Can you help me for a while?"

"Certainly; get him dressed and I'll take him with me to the airport."

"He loves airplanes. He will be delighted," was the quick response, and I could sense some relief.

I went to the door and said, "Jason, do you want to go with me out to the airport to see the planes?"

His yes was loud and clear. With his hand in mine we walked to the car. I talked to him all the time we were driving. I couldn't understand much of his response, but he was chatting and happy. That feeling was with him as we greeted my guest and then went shopping at the mall. A time or two he walked without holding my hand. One time he came running to me trying to tell me that he had seen the Easter bunny. He was very excited as he called to me, but we were too late. The bunny had gone on down the mall and into another store. It didn't matter. Jason had seen him and was so delighted with the experience that he just kept trying to tell me about Easter.

Jason was so good. It was a very special pleasure to have him with me. I was enriched that day to see a happy mother and a happy child. It was such a pleasure to share my grandson with my friend on that day.

I was serving as the general president of the Relief Society when Steven was born. His birthday was on the day we celebrated the Relief Society's organization. It was a very special experience to hold this newest grandson on a day so filled with the remembrance of the founding of Relief Society. Perhaps it was my preoccupation with the great power for good Relief Society has been in the lives of faithful women of the Church that made me think about the significant influence for good that mothers can have who dedicate themselves to nurturing and rearing their children with the gospel light.

I had, in fact, been thinking of the consecration of the baby boy of Sarah Melissa Granger Kimball. She was the first woman who thought of organizing the women into a society to help build the kingdom of God upon the earth. I remembered the promises that were made to her because of her dedication to the Lord and his work. (See A. Crocheron, *Representative Women of Deseret* [Salt Lake City: J. C. Graham and Co., 1884], pp. 24–28.)

The Saints were in the process of building the temple in Nauvoo, Illinois, according to counsel they had received from the Lord. Most of them had given up or spent their money when they joined the Church, and yet the Church was in desperate need of their financial support.

When the request for help came, Sarah Kimball tried to determine what she could give to the cause. She could have asked her husband, Hyrum, to make a contribution, but he was not a member and she wanted the contribution to be hers, not his. This matter weighed heavily upon her. She was expecting a new baby at the time, and when the baby was three days old she was given inspiration.

When her husband came to the bedside and was gazing at their new son she asked, "How much is the boy worth?"

"Oh, lots," exclaimed the new father.

"Is he worth a thousand dollars?" Sarah inquired.

"Yes, and more than that if he lives and does well."

"Half of him is mine, isn't it?" she pursued the discussion.

"Well, I suppose so!" was the father's answer.

"Good. Then I have something of my own to give to the Church. I'll give my half of the baby."

Surprised, Hyrum answered, "We'll see about that."

The next time he saw the Prophet Joseph Smith he told him about the conversation. The Prophet smiled and said, "Thank you. We accept all such offerings. You now have your choice, you can either give us $500 and retain possession of the boy or we will give you $500 and take possession of him."

The baby's father thought just a moment before he said, "Would you be satisfied if I deeded to you that piece of property just behind the temple lot?"

The Prophet smiled again and responded, "That is exactly what I had in mind."

The next time the Prophet saw Sarah Kimball he said, "Because you have consecrated your firstborn son to the Lord, you will be blessed and your name will go down in honorable remembrance from generation to generation."

Of course, this new grandson was not mine to give nor to consecrate to the service of the Lord. Still, I could think of nothing sweeter than to have a child consecrated to the Lord to bring forth the blessings of mortality for the mother and for generations yet to come. Steven's day of birth made it seem that he would have such a life, or could have if those of us with influence upon him helped him realize his own potential in this regard.

Victor Hugo said, "To reform a man, you must begin with his grandmother." Perhaps the building of a man whose life would be filled with understanding for women and consecrated to the sacred work of the Lord might also begin with his grandmother as she exerts an influence for good in his life.

Steven's fifth birthday came on the day when the governor of the state of Utah was to sign a proclamation declaring that April should be dedicated as the month to call special attention to preventing child abuse. I had been asked to serve in this challenging work. At the signing we hoped to have people from many organizations, people of many religious persuasions, people young and old. I called and invited Steven's mother to bring him so that he might begin that birthday celebration by participating in this moment of community dedication. I told the governor it was Steven's birthday, and he graciously sat for one more picture in his long picture-taking session—this one with Steven.

That day Steven had another special, enriching experience. I hope some day he will understand and let these special experiences help him grow. Hopefully exposures like these will enlarge his view of life and increase his dedication. One dedicated life can mean much to this world in which so few feel the willingness to take determined action to right wrongs.

The feedback from grandchildren gives one many thoughtful moments and sometimes helps grandmothers rearrange their priorities.

Here is a description of a grandmother as seen by one grandchild:

A grandmother is a lady who has no children of her own, so she likes other people's little girls. A grandfather is a man grandmother. He goes for walks with the boys, and they talk about fishing and tractors and [stuff] like that.

Grandmas don't have to do anything except be here. They're old, so they shouldn't play hard or run. It is enough if they drive us to the market where the pretend-horse is and have plenty of dimes ready. Or if they take us for walks they should slow down past things like pretty leaves or caterpillars. They should never, ever say "Hurry up."

Usually, they are fat, but not too fat to tie kids' shoes. . . . They can take their teeth and gums off.

It is better if they don't typewrite or play cards except with us. They don't have to be smart, only answer questions like why dogs hate cats and how come God isn't married. They don't talk baby talk like visitors do because it is so hard to understand. When they read to us, they don't skip or mind if it is the same story again.

Everybody should try to have one grandmother, especially if you don't have television, because grandmas are the only grownups who have got time. (From *Especially for Mormons*, Vol. 2 [Provo, Utah: Kellirae Arts, 1973], p. 120.)

There are limitations to a child's perception of a grandmother, but this child did identify one marvelous truth: Most of us as grandmothers have just enough time to bring some edification and enrichment into the lives of our grandchildren, whether through a trip, a talking session in which some things are clarified, or a concert to extend our feeling for the good and the beautiful.

One of the great human needs, our society is finding out, is the need for time one on one. It is very rewarding and enriching for grandmothers to spend some of that time with grandchildren. The enrichment that comes to us as well as to our grandchildren may be limitless. It's one of the things that makes life worth living.

Neglect not the gift that is in thee.
— 1 Timothy 4:14

CHAPTER NINE

Growing with Talents

Reading to a four-year-old granddaughter was a sweet experience for me. It was interesting to see her watch each word as we read *Little Women* together. I realized very soon that she was checking to see that I didn't miss a word on the page. Finally I asked, "Why don't you read to me for a while?"

"I can't read the words. They are too little for me."

"You can try," I encouraged. She began and she hardly missed a word. (She did need a little help, but just a very little bit.) It was a thrill to watch that bright little mind bring to bare all of her thinking processes as she enjoyed the story she was reading. It was just a glimpse into the possibilities of her life.

It set me thinking about another facet of a grandmother's life. It is true that the child's fundamental training was being given by her mother and father. I knew that her parents had given her some understanding of words, and I knew too that she had listened to some of the children's television programs on which phonetics were taught. Yet I also knew that my encouragement could scoot her even further along a learning path. She had doubts about her ability to read the little print, and she had the notion that a four-year-old child was too young to read. With just those words "You can try," many of the negatives were wiped away. Then she succeeded and that gave her the confidence that she could continue.

It was an exciting moment.

It is a constant wonderment to me to be brought face to face with the capabilities and talents of my children and grandchildren. It gives me renewed hope for the world. If they can be encouraged to develop their full potential, then I am sure the world's problems, however knotty and tangled, will be worked out as time goes by. It may be true that new problems will come. Nevertheless, my faith in the human soul is not bounded by the negatives I see.

Parents must provide the first training, just as they provide the home and the pattern of the home. But there is an important place for grandparents in encouraging the development of talents. This they should not neglect.

The grandparent can sit and listen while the first-time reader gets his or her practice. The grandmother can cheer on her grandson in athletic competitions. The grandmother can see and appreciate a beginner's sculpturing. The grandmother can recognize talents not always visible to a performance-oriented world and give appreciation and encouragement.

The invincible attitude of a child needs to be encouraged if talents are to be developed. Once I heard Barbara, aged nine, say to her mother, "I think I should study the harp, the piano, the violin, take ballet lessons, and study a foreign language." At first I thought all of that sounded very ambitious. Then I realized that she needn't do all of those things at once, but in proper sequence they could all enrich her life and she would soon be able to determine the real direction her ambitions should take.

I'm not certain, however, that she was thinking in one-at-a-time terms. She went up to the concert pianist in her ward the next Sunday and asked, "Do you have time to take me as a piano student?" Surprised, the musician responded, "I really don't have time right now, but if you can wait until spring I think I can fit you into my schedule.'' ''Thank you,'' she said. ''I'll be waiting to hear from you.''

What a thrill it is to see her quick, astute mind consider very thoroughly her plans and then put them into immediate action. Just being around her is an exciting experience.

I can't help but think that her cousin Amy will be very much like her. Amy is very precocious at three years of age. The attributes of kindness, gentleness, and creativity are obvious. She likes to invite her grandmothers into her room. When she closes the door, her imagination opens more doors than I can believe. She prepares pretend food, shops for it, discusses the smells and flavors, her likes and dislikes. She involves her many dolls in the world she creates. A power glorious in form and brilliance took me immediately into the beautiful land of fantasy. I hope Amy can forever hold tight to the real as well as to the vision of possibility.

Becky Lou, the eldest in her family, has one of those not-so-visible talents. She has the ability to nurture her younger brothers. In developing this talent she has had to overcome some disappointments, but she has done so and developed the virtue of kindness besides.

Being the eldest in the family has its advantages and its disadvantages. The advantages include the realization that the oldest is also generally wiser than any of the other children. The disadvantages are multiple. One is that, when you decide you want a little sister, you have no control over what happens. In fact, Becky Lou had six opportunities to have a little sister. With each birth came the telephone call that said, ''You have another little baby brother.'' There was always that hope. It would have been funny if Becky hadn't wanted a baby sister so desperately. But the babies were so beautiful that when they came home from the hospital they were loved and accepted and there was immediately a breath of special affection which was only magnified when the little one was placed in his big sister's arms. She knew she would help raise each baby brother. She would hold him when her mother was busy. She knew more and more the experience of finding unique traits in her brothers. She would spend time with each brother. She was the one who had to set a good example and help her brothers understand the rules of the family. Often, her parents asked her to plan family activities that would draw them together as a unit. She found she had a talent for doing this.

Quickly, with each new brother, she put her desire for a little sister into proper perspective. The important thing was the individual. She soon appreciated the fact that the Lord had given the family the little spirit who would be best for them. So Becky loved and gratefully welcomed Nathan, Daniel, Benjamin, Jacob, Paul, and Andrew. As a matter of fact, she grew to like boys and the place that was hers alone in the family—that of being the only girl and enjoying the love and respect a one-of-a-kind receives.

Jacob has another talent. Like so many of our grandsons, he is absolutely thrilled with basketball. Perhaps it is inherited from his father or his uncles or his grandfathers, who were all interested in the sport. Maybe it skipped through some generations from his great-grandfathers who enjoyed and played the game as well.

In any case, Jacob is an aggressive little player. He has learned how to dribble and to shoot. He has been taken to games almost from the time he was born. First, as a little boy, he just watched from the bleachers, but now he has begun to participate. Soon he will be playing with the junior league; who knows what the next step up will be? Jacob seems to make good use of the energy that drives him as he participates in sports. He is pleased when we come and watch him play in his competitive games. Learning how to develop one's body and coordination and sportsmanship is part of the education that develops the whole child. Innate abilities can emerge even at a very young age.

Part of the joy Jacob finds in developing his athletic skills is the companionship of kindred people. Part of it is the instant approval from the spectators when he makes a good play. Part of it is being his best. He's learning, and we are excited to see him developing good sportsmanship. He is learning that sometimes you lose in sports and sometimes in life.

Giving him the encouragement he needs will spur in him the

enthusiasm to move forward in life with excitement. He will come to understand others who feel as he does and have the courage to stand equally as strong in the game of life. There will be many fouls called as he interacts with people, but he will know more of the venturesome life if he can move forward knowing that there are rules in basketball as well as in life. His earnestness and zeal in playing this game should be of great worth in his life. We will be there to cheer him on in both places.

How often I have thought, *I was there to help my grand-children learn the lesson.* I know that is true, but now slowly I am beginning to see that through them my understanding of life and its experiences is enlarging. Their lives and mine have great parallels.

Leslie is another grandchild who has been given some athletic talent. Her natural talent emerged to delight her grandparents and her family in the world of swimming competition. She wasn't like her sisters. She knew that. She was her own person, an individual with abilities and talents unlike anyone else's in the family, and she wanted to prove it. From her first experience in the water of the neighborhood swimming pool, she felt if she worked hard and long enough she could become a part of the team.

Fortunately, good people were organizing the programs, people willing to teach young children how to develop the necessary physical strength in their arms and legs as well as the techniques to become very good swimmers and capable competitors in swimming meets. Leslie was a very determined little girl, and she did the things that were required of her. She ate what she needed to eat. She practiced hours upon hours, forcing herself to go beyond her comfort zone. She entered the meets and at first found herself behind the others as the races finished. But she was committed to success. That pleased me. Her mother kept telling her to do her best without worrying about anyone else in the race. When she found that she could take that first step, she was pleased. She made up her mind that she would work hard and improve until she would not only finish the race —she would also finish it ahead of at least one other swimmer. She practiced with more zeal. She believed in her potential. She was determined to develop and watched herself not only passing other swimmers but finding that her efforts soon brought her into the winner's circle.

She was always so pleased when her grandparents were there cheering with the other members of her family. Grandmothers can become a very good cheering section. There is something about the way their voices carry across the water . . . at least Leslie seemed to hear mine.

To stimulate learning, we have found it fun while riding in the car to memorize poems, scriptures, or just trivia. Some of the children remember the lines surprisingly quickly, while others can do it if we develop a rhythm pattern, a beat, or put the information to familiar music. For example, learning the books of the New Testament or the number of days in the month becomes easier in song. It is always amazing to me to see how quickly children can acquire skills and knowledge.

It has been a source of great excitement to note the very real differences in our grandchildren's talents and the diversity with which they move forward, especially when grandparents listen or encourage them.

Grandparents can help children understand the need to discipline their talents and thus liberate the gifts they have been given. I watched Andrea, that bright four-year-old reader, accept and carry through with a housekeeping task. She did it with such speed that it almost made one dizzy, and it was well done. She is a perfectionist with herself and with everyone else as well.

This child was given a few piano lessons, but like most little girls she hated to practice. She quit taking lessons. The tragedy was that quitting limited her natural gift severely so that she could not develop the talent within her.

When she entered junior high school something happened that touched her, and she wanted to play the piano. Now it was virtually impossible to get her away from the piano. She played it as soon as she came in from school and continued up to and almost through the dinner hour; and then she played it from early evening until bedtime. No one tried to stop her.

Now she is in high school and listening to counsel . . . at least she is listening a little. She found a teacher she thought would be good and then went for her first lesson. The teacher pointed out that she could play, which she knew, but in order to develop good techniques necessary for perfection, she would have to start all over again. We've been talking, and she has been exposed to the idea that this might be a great challenge. But she must impose some limits on herself and on the number of lessons she will take from the teacher. If then she faithfully strives for perfection in her playing, she can evaluate herself to see if the teacher really is offering her an enlarged opportunity to excellence.

She has an advantage as she begins because she comes from a family of perfectionists. It is a tradition. She has every opportunity to be the best. I reminded her that her father stayed an extra year to do a fellowship in ophthalmology so that he could perfect his skills and be better than ordinary. She might follow that same pattern and work to be more than just one of the bunch who can sit down and stumble through a musical score.

She listened.

Seeing her progress as she puts her heart, might, mind, and strength into the project is one of the real miracles of this life. What power in a young person! What possibilities yet to be developed! What a joy to be part of that growth and see it unfold!

The new computer technology has exposed new talents in our family. Hopefully, the new technology will bring solutions to many age-old problems. Handicaps of many kinds are being compensated for by computer-aided technology, making it possible for some blind to see and some who cannot hear to hear again and some who cannot speak to express themselves.

Computer technology is just part of living for some of our grandchildren. Douglas is already amazing. He is a young master at video games and in the process is mastering his computer. He loves to take anyone on who comes to visit, especially his grandparents. No matter how hard I try, I cannot outplay him. He has skills and abilities that are amazing to see. He takes something that looks hard and complicated and turns it into something that to him is simple and fun. To this young grandson the coming decade will be a joy and a never-ending challenge. Developments in the world of technology will take place, and he will quickly move into that world of wonders. While most of us are wondering about the computer revolution, he will be there participating fully well ahead of the rest of us. He is already cultivating those skills that he will need. I can only begin to glimpse the world he will know. I really cannot imagine what will come when his talents are fully utilized.

Just to live in this age of mechanical marvels is amazing, but to watch a child fit so easily into it, to watch him grow by leaps and bounds as he absorbs the technical advancements of our day helps me to realize that this generation and the next will grow into areas of knowledge that defy my understanding.

George Santayana said that "the wisest mind hath something yet to learn."

Recognizing and encouraging our grandchildren to develop their talents leaves me with the realization that the process is always folding back on itself. Grandchildren encourage grandparents to keep learning and developing, too.

One of the great blessings of being a grandparent is constant stimulation from grandchildren to keep learning and developing one's own talents. Growth comes to the individual in tiny strokes of dedicated practice. It also comes in leaps and bounds as new things unfold and understanding dawns. In all my interactions with my grandchildren, even when I am being most helpful, I realize with humility that I am growing and learning more than I am giving. It is a sobering thought.

Be thou an example of the believers, in word, in conversation, in charity, in spirit, in faith, in purity.

—1 Timothy 4:12

CHAPTER TEN

Growing Through Values

There is a church in New England that celebrates what they call "Ancestors' Day." On that day the people put on costumes appropriate to the particular ancestors from whom they claim their descent. They recall the deeds, reenact the ideals, and relive the faith of their ancestors. They do this to recall some of the peoples of the past and give them reverence for excellence of character or praiseworthy quality in the lives of those who are the object of their wholehearted admiration. Elder Sterling W. Sill reports that on this special day the people of this church turn their thoughts to the abilities and characteristics they have inherited. They also remember with fondness the helpful training they have received that starts them on their way in the world. (See Sterling W. Sill, *Leadership*, vol. 2 [Bookcraft, 1960], p. 23.)

Interestingly enough, the good effects of this devotion extend in both directions. When we focus this loving, reverent attention on someone or something, we tend to be transformed into the likeness of the thing we love.

It is a refining and uplifting experience to recognize those who have gone before us and left us a heritage of righteousness. It may take years before we mature enough to know what has directed our lives. For example, when my parents took us each Sunday to visit our grandparents, Grandfather and Grandmother Bradshaw would insist that we sit down to supper at their table filled with homegrown food. We talked about their garden and admired the biggest turnips, longest parsnips, and crispest orange carrots that were just bulging with goodness and then tasted the homemade bread and onions and cheese with the ice cold milk spread before us. My eyes were wide with admiration that anyone could make the ground produce food like that. I gained a profound appreciation for the law of the harvest, although it never occurred to me to refer to it in that way. As a little girl what I appreciated was the bounteous food. But now I remember most a strength and a oneness that I felt when I was there, a sweet, bonding feeling that persisted as long as my grandmother and grandfather were there together. The seeds that made the vegetables grow were not very different from the seeds of love and faith and strength that were engendered in all who sat at that table.

One woman told me that as a child she sat with her brothers and sisters and parents around the kitchen table long after the meal was over. Here the children received the full attention of their mother. She was a listening audience and she wanted to know from them what had taken place during the day. She listened and philosophized with her children about life and its purposes.

I believe that was what happened at the table of my grandparents. They were a wonderful listening audience. They wanted to share our accomplishments with us. They liked to hear about our joys, our difficulties, and our problems. Around their table we rejoiced in caring and direction from those who had lived long and well enough to give us wise counsel.

As I look back now at so many shared experiences, I am aware that many of the values I hold dear were passed along to me from my parents and grandparents through shared experiences.

Albert Schweitzer is reported to have said: "If you would make a difference in the life of a child, three things are important. The first is example, the second is example, and the third is example." He went on to say, "Example is not the most important thing, it is the only thing."

When I think about it, I realize that my experiences with my grandparents reinforced every value teaching I ever received from my mother and father. This made it easier to make those values my own.

Grandmother Bradshaw never mentioned this mistake to me, but I never forgot it. She had left me, a little girl, to "watch the baking bread and take it from the oven when it browns . . . probably about forty-five minutes," I was told. The bread wasn't brown in forty-five minutes, nor in one hour and forty-five minutes. When she came home the fire was out and the bread was still in the oven. I suppose it was then she realized that I had never had experience with a coal stove. I wasn't criticized for my mistake. I learned that bread won't bake without a fire. But far more significant to me was her example: she cared about my feelings. She could have been angry about the bread but instead taught me a lesson of love for people and concern for their feelings that will forever guide me.

I was just as fortunate with my maternal grandmother. She had taken Mother and us children with her to visit relatives in Wyoming. Nana, as we called her, had one of the few new cars in the area, and we were happy to ride anywhere with her. As we left the cousins at the first home, I hopped into the car and slammed the door after me. There was a cry of pain and a request to please open the door. As I did I saw the expression of anguish on Nana's face. She held her poor smashed fingers while uncontrollable tears trickled down her cheeks—but with never a word of condemnation. She knew it was an accident. She seemed to sense the suffering of my soul. I loved her so very much, I couldn't bear to think I had hurt her. Her stoic bearing remains with me as a constant reminder that the children of God are here to learn the hard lessons as well as the joyful ones. Pain can be borne and love can be shown, and a little girl can be buoyed up and not destroyed by a hurtful attack.

I cannot think of anything I value highly that is not insepar-
ably connected with my grandparents and their great example.

Perhaps the first thing I remember clearly as a family value
was to value my family. From my earliest days my parents took
us to family gatherings. Who could forget the joyful gathering
of the Bradshaw clan for Thanksgiving dinner? It now reminds
me of the song "Over the River and Through the Woods,"
except we didn't go by sleigh. Looking up and down that
wonderful, full table in my grandmother's house, seeing heap-
ing plates of good food, listening to the laughter of the men as
they cleaned up the dishes, and feeling happy and well loved
as the family joined in singing around the piano gave me a warm
and wonderful feeling of love.

The annual Christmas trek from home to home was not a
chore. It was eagerly awaited as part of the festivities, for we
were going to see the families that we loved.

These glowing memories have motivated me often to gather
my own children and grandchildren together to share a meal,
to talk together, to listen to each other perform, and to build
continuing memories.

I value family and family ties.

Another family value that I now have made my own is a testimony of the gospel of Jesus Christ as it has been restored to us
in its fullness. Sometimes my grandparents and other grandparents I have known clearly demonstrated acceptance of individual principles. Sometimes I saw in action their testimonies
of the entire gospel.

In every case the interactions I had with my grandparents
were always more compelling when they were gospel-related.
Often, even when our experiences together didn't seem to be
gospel-related at the time, they soon became so for me, not only
with my own family but also with my husband's family as well.

Doug's grandparents shared with us some remarkable experiences that continue to sustain our faith and values. Once
Grandfather Smith was ill in the hospital for a number of
months. It was a fast and testimony Sunday when my father-in-
law, then a teenaged boy, returned home from priesthood meeting to find his mother in tears. When he asked her what the
problem was, she said, "I must pay our tithing, but if I do there

will be no money to buy fruit to bottle for our food this winter. If I don't pay my tithing, I won't have any claim upon the blessings of the Lord. Quickly—reach up on the top shelf for the cream pitcher, get the money, and run and give it to the bishop before I change my mind.'' Her young son did as he was told. The next morning she found on the front porch a fifty-pound bag of sugar and two bushels of the most beautiful peaches she had ever seen.

After a wind storm later that night, a neighbor called on the telephone and said, ''Sister Smith, we have many windfallen peaches. If you and your children would like to come and pick them up, you can have all you want.'' They had more peaches that year than ever before. Grandmother Smith was always anxious to share with her family the great lesson she learned that night regarding the principle of tithing. We continue to share her testimony of that miracle with our children and our grandchildren.

Another story, this one about Grandfather Smith, has always been a blessing to us. Grandfather Smith loved flowers. For many years he spent countless happy hours planting and cultivating them and arranging the patterns and colors. He even bought a lot adjoining his in order to grow more flowers. Groups of school children would come every spring to see his tulips and learn about the bulbs and how the blossoms grew. Grandfather Smith was proud of his work, and so was everyone in the neighborhood.

At tithing settlement time soon after Grandfather Smith retired, he found himself without money to contribute as tithing to the Church. That worried him a lot. He looked at his garden and determined to dig up every bulb, package them all, and sell them. Then he would have the money for tithing. He was almost heartbroken as he dug the bulbs up, but he thought he would rather live with only memories of that garden and remain faithful to a commitment he had made to himself always to be listed as a full tithe payer on the records of the Church. He felt a deep sense of satisfaction when the work had been completed, the bulbs sold, and the money paid to the bishop.

Grandfather Smith didn't look forward to spring that year. He knew a bleak and barren plot of ground would greet him as he surveyed his former garden. To his surprise and delight he had just as many tulips that spring as he had had before he dug the bulbs. His lesson has been shared with the family many times. We learned to value the payment of tithes.

Many examples of devoted service in the Church make up part of the heritage that has been passed on to me. From the beginning our marriage has been enriched by the opportunities for service that have come to us. It was so from the day Elder Mark E. Petersen asked me if I could support my husband in his calling as a bishop to the day President Spencer W. Kimball asked Doug if he could support me in my calling as general president of the Relief Society. We have found Church service—given willingly and with an open heart—to be of great value.

When Doug was called to be a bishop it was necessary for him to reorganize the entire ward because the old ward had been divided. As we watched people grow in the dedicated service they gave, we came to a new understanding of the encouragement our parents and grandparents had always given us to be dedicated in our service. It is a value we would pass on for the growth it brings.

After a lifetime of response to Church callings, I begin to see that it has all been a preparation for our "grandparenting" years. I say this because I see that the lessons we learned are so significant that we must pass them on to the children who follow us; their devotion to service will thus open their lives to love in a much more meaningful way than otherwise possible.

We have learned to appreciate the priesthood, to teach, to put away offended feelings, to find balance in our lives, to listen to criticism, and to school our quick feelings; in short, we have learned much about working with many people. This makes us better able to listen and counsel our loved ones without destroying their agency.

Our Church experiences also give us a reservoir of spiritual strength from which to draw to provide love and support to ourselves as well as to others. One grandmother I know said she wanted to be "prayed up" all the time so that she could always feel comfortable in going to the Lord in time of need.

Another grandmother told me the story of her son, who is a photographer in San Francisco for the news media. He had found living expenses to be exorbitant, so he and his wife decided they would buy a houseboat and live on it with their four children. He looked over boat after boat until he found the one that seemed perfect for them. After making the down payment on it, he went to get it with the help of his wife's father and brothers, the skipper, and his older friend. As they brought the boat into the bay, a sudden storm came up, and waves twelve to fifteen feet high broke the ship into lumber. They manned a rubber life raft and notified the Coast Guard that they needed help. From 8:30 P.M. until 4:00 A.M. the next morning no one really knew what was happening to them. As soon as the grandmother was notified of the problem, she drove down to be with her daughter-in-law. As she arrived, the Coast Guard had someone there and they were listening with her daughter-in-law for any news of the boat. Soon the Coast Guard station reported finding a raft and people alive on it. The daughter-in-law's mother heard the report that an older man was dead, and she assumed it was her husband. They eventually found out it was the friend of the skipper, who said he was too old to survive the experience and would not cooperate or help; he simply gave up. The rubber raft had capsized three or four times, and they were able to get their group back into it. After the first time they thought the older man was dead. The next time it took all of their strength, and the third time they could not get him aboard. So they took his life jacket and gave it to one of the more active men who didn't have one.

The experience was emotional and very difficult, but throughout it the daughter-in-law seemed almost angelic in her appearance and attitude. However, when it was over she and her own mother had spent all of their optimism and courage. When the little children began to cry hysterically, she called her mother-in-law to come back again and help. She said, "I just can't handle it alone." The tantrums reached hysteria. The mother-in-law talked calmly and tried to read stories to keep the children from thinking about the experience, but it took time. She did all she could, but she also let the troubled children kick and scream. The grandmother was concerned that she might not be handling the situation the way her daughter-in-law would like her to. She asked her about it: "I know we have different religious beliefs, and I do want to offer comfort to the children. What do you want me to say to them?''

The answer was, ''Feel free to say whatever you believe will be helpful.'' Then the grandmother dipped into her own full well. She knew the stories of the scriptures, told them to her grandchildren, and prayed for peace and a calmness of spirit to come to the four-year-old and to the older children who were so deeply affected.

Soon one of the grandchildren was asking, ''Would you tell me another true story of what happened to the children of our Heavenly Father?'' or ''Will you tell me a true story about our ancestors?'' And one time when there was a conversation about someone who had a tragic death in their family, the oldest child said, ''It's all right. She will get her body back again.''

This grandmother found ways to help her grandchildren gain an eternal perspective through the stories of the scriptures and of her grandparents and others who had gone before. To bring the spirit of calmness and peace from the scriptures to her loved ones was a matter of great significance to the grandmother. ''When I was a little girl, my grandmother used to do this,'' she would say to her grandchildren. They would reply, ''Well, if your grandma did that to you, you can do it to me.''

Education is another value highly prized in our family. My grandmother was in the first graduating class of the Brigham Young Academy. She was one of Karl G. Maeser's early students, and she always had a great appreciation and admiration for Dr. Maeser. She said that he always explained that they were to be good students. She spent most of her time really trying to become that kind of a student. He was a strong prod to all of the students in that first class, and most of them became outstanding professional people. My grandmother went east to study medicine after she was married and had given birth to three children. She had the full support of her husband in her studies.

My mother was a capable schoolteacher before her marriage. Her parents had valued education so much that they moved to Salt Lake City when Mother was a young child so that she could get her schooling. She was selected from among all the local high school students to read the dedicatory prayer for the Seagull Monument on Temple Square.

Grandchildren often feel encouraged to continue their schooling when they sense the deep commitment to learning which has preceded them. Family traditions in education have plainly manifested themselves among the grandchildren. It is helpful when this great legacy is shared with those whom the children marry.

Education Week was a highlight in our family. It was fun to ride together to wherever the program was being held and talk about the classes we planned to attend. On the way home, our discussions of all that we had learned were stimulating. We talked about ways to use the information to enrich our Church assignments and the lives of our family members. Our attendance might have been encouraged by a calling to teach a class, but the whole feeling increased as we talked about ways the learning would be influential in many lives.

Honesty is a character trait upon which I place great value; but I never really thought about it until one day in junior high school. The school paper came out with a list of traits of many of the students. By the name of Barbara Bradshaw the editors had listed the word *honesty*. I remember thinking that if people thought of me in that way, I must always be honest. This made me desire to be strictly honest in all my dealings.

It was, therefore, with deeply poignant feelings that I listened to my granddaughter Allison recount with tears in her eyes a severely disappointing experience at her school. She is a good student, and her teacher had asked her to keep the record of math home assignments as they were turned in.

Pleased by the trust placed in her, she was very honest in her record keeping. Then one day a classmate offered her a one-dollar bill if she would put a mark by his name indicating that he had turned in an assignment even though he hadn't. Allison said she couldn't do what he asked. Later he caught her eye and offered her twenty dollars for that one little mark by his name. She shook her head, and the day crept along to the final bell. After school she got into the car full of her friends that her mother was driving. She told her mother about this experience while the other young people listened. Then they began to laugh and tell her how dumb she was. They said, "Even the teacher would have put the mark by his name for twenty dollars." Then there was more ridiculing. She thought she would find acceptance of her action among these friends since she knew that most of them had been taught the same fundamental values she had been taught. She had not been sorely tempted by the money but was offended at the idea of cheating. In the car, however, she felt ridiculed for her honesty, and that really hurt. In the difficult world in which we live today, our grandchildren will need our support to maintain their fundamental values.

Hard work with a good spirit and a happy face were other fundamental values of my home. My children's grandmother, my mother, never approached a task without the happy anticipation of the challenge it presented.

"Anybody," she used to say, "can prepare a meal if they have plenty of money to buy whatever they want. But it is a real accomplishment to make a nutritional meal out of what is on hand." She would go merrily about the task of preparing a meal with whatever was in our basement storage. Prepared quick-mixes were not available then, but she did the quickest mixing I have ever seen, and what she whipped up was always wonderful.

When I was a teenager, a boyfriend came to visit me, but my mother needed my help peeling peaches. She said that I couldn't go with him just then, but if he would like to stay he could help us bottle the fruit. He was willing, she gave him a paring knife, and we were soon busily engaged. She made it fun. It was her conversation that was captivating—her wit and her wisdom. We learned and laughed and the work was done.

When Mother would come each week in her later years for me to set and comb her hair, she always wanted to help with the household chores in payment for the time it required. Of course, it was my privilege to have her come, but she would enlist the help of one child and then another and together they would laugh and learn until that work was all done. We all looked forward to her visits. Mother had a special way of including people. It didn't matter if it was housework, errands, or entertainment, she wanted us with her; and we loved to know that we were an important part of her life.

I know a grandmother who acknowledges that the road to happiness is always under construction, but even the detours can make it an interesting experience to be enjoyed. Sometimes it is the detours that bring the interesting and character-building results. That was the feeling we had with Mother.

Today's world would not be suffering from what might be called an ethics crisis if we had more people like those who have taught me values. Recently Wall Street has had to face up to a serious scandal concerning the inappropriate use of "insider" information. Experts discussing the problem pointed to the lack of a sufficient sense of ethics among the participants in the scandal, and they turned to the prestigious business schools to ask if they taught ethics. "Yes," was the reply, but the teaching and practicing of ethics must take place on a continuum that spans a lifetime. Short-term gains must be put into an appropriate context with ethical conduct and the long-term building of a life.

In the reinforcement of the child's first insights and in the first effort to apply ethical teachings in the world outside the family, the grandmother will find great challenges. One grandchild declared: "My grandmother was the heart of our home. She was the original spiritual source. She was the warm accepting sounding board and my haven. If Grandmother said anything was right, it was. As children we accepted whatever she said. She will probably never know of the great impact she had upon my life. She was a rule reinforcer. She always backed Mother up. I suppose that was one of the strengths of having her there close by and knowing what we were doing as children."

Another said: "Our grandmother had rules. The rules were the same as we had in our home, so it wasn't different going to Grandmother's house. Her life was one of spiritual enrichment rather than discipline. We found her often going around and rescuing those that began to stray. She cared for my daughter during the nine months of my divorce. I will never underestimate the good that she did in saving my child."

Any help which grandmothers can give to keep alive the simple old character traits upon which all ethics are based is an essential contribution. Most often it will come through reinforcement of the home rules. A grandmother's standing up for the right gives strength. One child reported that she thought her grandmother's gentle way of saying "I'm proud to see you behave that way" was the strength of her life.

A special friend tells me that she spent many hours with her grandmother, and those hours shaped her life. When she was about ten, she and her grandmother spent many hours looking for rocks. They knew that geodes were to be found in the Bear River area, and it would be fun to find some. As they looked they began to see rocks that were beautifully colored, rocks with unusual shapes, rocks whose surfaces seemed to have a story to tell. There were rocks of so many kinds that the search was a fascination to both of them. Whenever they traveled to different places they always looked for a rock they could bring back to share with each other. This was not a momentary pastime but an intensive effort. Sometimes they would have the rock cut and formed to the shape they could see in it. Other times they wouldn't let anyone mar the rock.

One time my friend was visiting her grandmother and walked with other family members into the nearby hills. There she found a rock that was different and unique, one that she simply had to bring home for the rock collection. It was really too big to carry by herself and no one wanted to be bothered to help her. She carried it until she couldn't carry it any farther. She put it on the ground and pushed it along with her foot. On a slope she would give it a fairly good push, and it would slide quite far by itself. When she finally got it home, her grandmother said, "I can't believe you had the tenacity to bring that big rock all the way home. That was hard and required a lot of strength and determination. But," she added, "some things are worth that huge effort."

More years passed by and the grandmother became ill. She was so terribly sick that no one but herself thought she could possibly get well. When my friend visited with her and they both wept over her remarkable recovery, her grandmother said: "When things were the very worst I kept thinking about that big rock you brought home from the mountains. I would say to myself, 'My granddaughter did it. She struggled hard to get the rock home. She had the strength and the determination. I can do it. This is one of those things that are worth every bit of effort I can put forth. There are still some things that I must do. I will get well.' "

They wept freely and openly together that day. They had learned the importance of being resolute. It let them share life together for a longer time.

It was even more years before many of her earthly possessions were divided among the family. My friend had the assurance that her grandmother's earthly possessions would be shared with all the members of the family. However, she felt fairly certain that the rock collection would be there, boxed and waiting for her. Each beautiful rock was a memory, a memory of time they had spent together seeing the beauty of the world, the beauty of life, and the beauty of character.

My young grandson Paul has begun to show evidence of a developing resolute courage. He could hardly wait for his entrance into kindergarten, but he was not thrilled when told about the physical and dental examinations that must precede it. He sat waiting in the dentist's office, and one could see his mounting tension. When the nurse said, "Paul, the doctor is ready for you now," his little body trembled nervously. His mother asked, "Do you want me to go with you?" It was a very serious little man who said, "No thank you, Mother. If I am big enough to go to school alone, I should be big enough to sit in the dentist's chair alone."

When we talked with Paul about that experience, he was more than pleased that we recognized great growth in that attitude.

One of my favorites among the sculptures in the monument to women is the one entitled "In Her Mother's Footsteps." It reminds me of my mother and the many other mothers I have met throughout the United States and around the world. They live lives filled with countless acts of kindness and love. It is in their little, nameless, almost unremembered acts of kindness and love that humanity is lifted to a higher level of experience. I know that my own soul is soothed and quieted and comforted when kind words are spoken, and I hope that my contribution to the lives of my grandchildren always will be made in such a way that they will remember some of those noble feelings that come with the refreshment of kind and caring words.

I see this quality of innate kindness in my granddaughter Sarah. Four brothers didn't seem to be too many for Sarah. In fact, to the youngest boy, Brian, Sarah seemed almost a second mother. She accepted the responsibility of loving and mothering him. She would change his diapers and feed him and carry him about. As she did these things, a sweetness of spirit came into her life. Love radiated from her. A mother loves her child in spite of difficult days, and so does Sarah love her brother. She was there to respond to Brian's first smile, his laugh, his first step. I don't mean to imply that no one else did those things, but a gentle bond of loving devotion arose between Sarah and her little brother as she followed willingly into the pathway set by her mother. The joyful thing was to see her developing traits of kindness and understanding as the fundamental building blocks of her character.

It is a good thing for grandmothers and grandfathers to give solid examples and constant encouragement to grandchildren that they may grow with solid characters acquainted with the comfort and the direction which comes from the Lord.

The way of the Lord is strength to the upright.
                    —Proverbs 10:29

CHAPTER ELEVEN

Growing in Spirituality

Of all the things I know about in this life, those which I value most are the things that I know through the Spirit. These things speak to me of an eternal bond between heaven and earth and are the things I most desire to pass on to my children and my grandchildren.

I believe a family is greatly strengthened by sharing in religious faith. I believe grandmothers can help reinforce the great significance of spiritual growth and development. There are some very natural times to share one's faith. The surprising thing to me is that after many decades of personal faith and long hours of service in Church callings, I am finding new depths in my own soul through the sharing of my faith with my grandchildren and participating with them during sacred moments.

It was at Easter time that two little boys were quarreling over whose father was the best. The one said, "My dad is a doctor and he can help people get well!" The other little boy retorted, "My dad is an auto mechanic and he can fix any car in this whole state!'' To which the first little boy said, ''Well, my grandma knows all about the Lord!''

It's not that grandmas know all about the Lord, but it's good that this little boy thought knowledge of the Lord was important, too; and it was comforting that he thought his grandmother was the expert.

For many grandmothers the hope that they can enrich their grandchildren's understanding of eternal things is of utmost significance. My mother used the occasion of Easter to talk to us about Jesus Christ. She made us hot cross buns, and as she put that little strip of frosting on each one we talked about the cross and the fact that Jesus was lifted up on the cross as told in the Book of Mormon:

> My Father sent me
> that I might be lifted up on the cross;
> and after that I had been lifted up
> upon the cross, that I might draw
> all men unto me,
> that as I have been lifted up
> by men even so should men be lifted up
> by the Father, to stand
> before me,
> to be judged of their works,
> whether good or evil—
> And for this cause have I been lifted up. (3 Nephi 27:14, 15.)

Years later when we tried to do the same thing for our children, my sister's daughter said, ''I can't believe you would put such a stingy little bit of icing on the hot cross bun.'' She had completely missed the purpose of the cross on the bun until she asked her own mother for the recipe for the hot cross buns. As she announced that she would certainly put more frosting on them than her mother had, my sister explained to her the significance of this tradition.

Nevertheless, parents and grandparents keep trying to help young minds fathom the significance of ideas that adults also struggle with—the meaning of the crucifixion and atonement of Jesus Christ and the reality of his resurrection.

It was just before Easter when Melissa announced to her mother, "I know that you [meaning her father and mother] are the Easter Bunny, the Tooth Fairy, and all those guys—except Santa Claus!" She was almost five years old and had been giving those things a lot of thought. She could not believe that a bunny could get down the chimney or hop into each house with its paws filled with Easter baskets, candy eggs, and Easter out-fits. It was not plausible to her little mind. Trying to save the excitement of the occasion for her, her father quickly asked, "Do I look like an Easter Bunny? Do I have long ears?" He found himself rolling with laughter at her innocent response, "Well, kinda!"

Trying to separate reality from fantasy in such a way that life can bring forth happiness and anticipation and yet teach the true meaning of days of religious celebration is a challenge and a blessing.

A friend told me that even though she never knew her grand-father, at Easter she always received some papier maché Easter eggs from him. They lifted her. She had so little that those Easter eggs gave her a feeling of being important. All of her friends wanted to see them and hold them and enjoy their beauty. Even the eggs she dyed at home were beautiful because of her other grandfather, who was a musical instrument maker. He would take the lacquer he used on the instruments and paint the eggs after they were dyed as beautifully as she could make them. These were exceptionally interesting to her friends, and each Easter she found herself the center of attention among her peers. She was lifted up because of Easter. She was very young when she learned the lesson Gandhi taught: "Divine guidance often comes when the horizon is the blackest." The Easter eggs were a symbol of that most divinely significant event, that gift of greatest love.

Jesus had been tried and tempted before he was crucified, and I know that each of us has or will have our times of trial. Each test that has come to me and to those I know and love the most has carried with it the elements of the Savior's tests and temptations—selfishness, pride in earthly possessions, power, glory, money, or personal aggrandizement, as well as physical or mental sufferings. The tests, whenever they come or whatever they are, force upon us this choice: Can we walk in faith and by strict obedience, or will we put aside the things of the Lord in favor of the earthly options offered by the great Tempter?

Much has been written and said about Mormon women and the priesthood. Little of the argumentative discussion over power and position reveals any insight into the heart of my faith in the power of the priesthood. My life has been touched many times by the power of a priesthood blessing, and I know my life is richer and more meaningful because the priesthood of God is upon the earth.

It is a comfort to know that my husband holds the priesthood and that he can perform the sacred blessings upon the sick when the need arises. When David was born with a club foot, I was filled with the overwhelming desire to have my son and his wife, new young parents, claim all of the marvelous blessings of the priesthood of God. I wanted them to draw close to each other and to the Lord. I wanted them to know that there was eternal strength available to them in this time of their sorrow and their need. I thought I had known joy before, but when Blaine turned to his father and said that night in the hospital, "Dad, let's give our baby boy a blessing," there welled up in me a feeling the like of which I had never experienced before. I knew they knew where to turn in times of need, and I knew that they had invited the most powerful healing power anywhere to be with their infant son.

Twelve Decembers passed. A telephone invitation came to gather for David's ordination to the priesthood. There were siblings, parents, and grandparents in the deacons quorum meeting that morning. It was a happy time and one that evoked many pent-up feelings of gratitude. David stood before his peers. He walked confidently, without a limp, to the circle of waiting priesthood holders. When they placed their hands on his head and by the authority given from Jesus Christ conferred the priesthood upon him, I felt tears of joy falling down my cheeks. How grateful I was for that first moment of decision when my son had assumed his role as a new father and faithfully turned to his Heavenly Father for a blessing. I had watched him and his wife for twelve years, and I knew that all of their efforts had been accompanied by faith and prayers for the divine healing influence to be with the boy and those who attended him. President Spencer W. Kimball said, "Boys need heroes close by." He also said, "Young men need fathers who set an example in leadership and who provide them with opportunities for development." (*Ensign*, May 1967, p. 45.) David had such a blessing.

The blessing of faith has come more than once to our family, and each time I've learned more of fathers, of mothers, of their faith, of courage, and of giving.

Catherine called one day and told us that her little son had a very high temperature. She asked if her father would come and help her husband give Joshua a blessing. Of course, he went immediately and I went with him. He walked right into the room to see that sick child and asked, "Joshua, have you ever had a blessing before?"

"Yes," he answered weakly. "Once before when I was sick my daddy put his hands on my ears and blessed me, and Heavenly Father made me well." I suppose that he could remember only those big hands on his little head pressing down on his ears. He did remember the experience. He received his priesthood blessing.

Early the next morning Catherine called to thank her father and said that very early Joshua had greeted them with a cheerful "Come and see. Heavenly Father has made me well again."

As I visited with a stake Relief Society president in California, she told me of a terrible accident that happened to her four-year-old granddaughter. The child had fallen from the window of her bedroom on the second story of the house. She had fallen onto a cement pavement below the room. Taken to the hospital, she remained in critical condition for weeks before she began to recover. Whenever she had a turn for the worse, she was given a priesthood blessing. As time went on she became well enough to go home. One day she was misbehaving and her grandmother asked, "What is the matter with you?" And the little girl replied, "I don't know. I guess I need a blessing." The message was relayed to her father. He gave her the blessing. She went about the house as happy as a lark.

The twenty-fourth of each December is a prescribed time for a family of my grandchildren to receive a father's blessing. Their father feels it is the most meaningful gift he can give to his children.

Little children learn very readily about spiritual things. When Joshua was just four he surprised us all at how deep an impression his healing blessings had made upon him. He asked the bishop if he might talk with him. The bishop said, "What do you want to talk with me about?" Joshua asked, "Could we go into your office?" When they arrived, there was someone else in the bishop's office, so the bishop asked Joshua, "Would it be all right with you if we talked together here in the clerk's office?" Joshua immediately agreed and then began his inquiry of the bishop. "Could you please tell me how Eric is feeling?" Eric was the bishop's son and Joshua's friend. The bishop replied, "He is a very sick little boy."

"Have you given him a blessing?" Joshua asked.

"No," answered the bishop. "We took him to the doctor, and we are giving him the medicine the doctor told us to give him."

"A blessing is better than medicine," said our grandson carefully. "Once when I was sick my daddy and my grandpa gave me a blessing and I was made well."

The bishop told me he felt reprimanded for not using the power of the priesthood. But most important was the fact that the child knew from those who loved him that the power was there to be used in his behalf.

The Lord said, "Come, follow me." He is abundantly creative; he invites, not commands, us to follow him. How many of us would refuse him if he invited us to sup with him? How many of us fail to follow him? He provides us with opportunities to serve and to learn. He assures us that we can magnify our callings. He describes our mission in this life and in the life to come. And he gives us the power to do his work and invites us to use the powers of heaven in our daily lives.

I think of this when I remember my granddaughter Jennie, because Jennie brings back memories of my involvement in the Donahue Show. I was on the Donahue Show because as president of the Relief Society I was seen as a spokeswoman for the women of the Church in response to pro-ERA groups that maligned us. I was anxious about the appearance on the TV show, and I was anxious for Jennie's mother. While Jennie was expected, her mother was having difficulties with high blood pressure and toxemia and was in the hospital as I left on a cold, snowy Sunday on the third of February. Catherine, her mother, had been given a blessing that she might be delivered of the baby and that all might be well. After her husband and mine had given her the blessing, I asked for one too. I was very anxious not to bring any embarrassment to the women I represented and loved.

I had an hour's wait as the plane had been delayed in the snowy weather. I was almost immediately transported to a meeting in the Chicago area with members of the Church, friends, and legislators. As I concluded my presentation, I mentioned the anxiety I felt over the forthcoming birth of a new grandchild. Prayers were offered for me and for the baby and the mother. When I returned to the hotel the light was flashing that indicated a call had come in. I returned the call to find that Jennie had been born. Her mother was fine. Jennie was in distress, but they had a very fine pediatrician working with her and felt that she would be all right.

The power of that blessing will always be of utmost importance to me. I believe the program went well. I know that Jennie had powers attending her that would have been unavailable without the priesthood there to bless her. I believe the priesthood blessing helped me meet that challenge of being on TV in a somewhat hostile environment as well.

President David O. McKay said: "What you sincerely in your heart think of Christ will determine what you are, will largely determine what your acts will be. . . . By choosing him as our ideal, we create within ourselves a desire to be like him." (Gospel Ideals [*Improvement Era,* 1953], pp. 34, 35.)

Nowhere do we have a greater need for this truth than in our marriage relations. The strength of the home, the strength of the nation, the strength of the eternal order of things depends upon men and women being able to respond to each other in a truly Christlike way.

One grandmother I know thinks that the relationship between a husband and wife can be enhanced if the mother or mother-in-law helps only when invited. She also teaches the idea that it is better for the couple not to find fault with each other. She believes that it is important to help a wife avoid taking over the mothering of a husband who has always been a child before his marriage. She thinks new wives should remember that both partners now begin a new life of opportunities, responsibilities, and adventures. They each have to make their own decisions as they talk together, plan together, and assume roles that are new and important to both of them. She feels that many people in marriage think, "If you are more, I am less." This is false, she says. We each need to learn to rejoice in what the other accomplishes. We need to respect our differences and grow from them. Their life together should be one of finding ways to make marriage work and to do it cooperatively. That new husband has been a son for twenty or more years. If doors are locked to his understanding of how to be a good husband, she helps find ways to get to him through the windows of peace and harmony.

This grandmother shares the ways she became a wife to her husband and not a mother. It was by praying that her Heavenly Father would help him to learn how to solve a particular problem. It did not come by her directing him in all his ways. She was always gratified when her husband would come up with decisions or suggestions that would help them learn how to work cooperatively toward a goal.

She told about a Relief Society president who always spent her time in thinking about how to run the Sunday School, or the Primary, or the Young Women's program and would always make so many suggestions to the bishop about these other organizations that he wearied of listening before she got to her ideas for the Relief Society. She suggests that each of us (including husbands and wives) would benefit and be infinitely more successful if we spent our time thinking about our own areas of responsibility and not try to direct others in theirs.

I believe grandmothers can initiate many plans to help bring added understanding of eternal things to their grandchildren. Jean Paul Richter observed: "As winter strips the leaves from around us, so that we may see the distant regions they formerly concealed, so old age takes away our enjoyments only to enlarge the prospects of the coming eternity." That may be why the significance of heavenly things is so clear to so many who are older—that and experiences like Katie's birth.

The weeks turned into months as Catherine waited in the hospital for her expected baby to grow big enough to live without the life-support systems required when a baby is born too soon. Catherine kept saying, "We simply can't afford the rising costs." The doctor replied, "This is cheap to what it will cost you if you deliver the baby too soon. It costs you about one hundred dollars a day compared to four hundred dollars a day if the baby needs special care for weeks and months in the intensive care units for premature infants." Catherine decided it was best for all concerned, but it was still very difficult to find peace when five children were left at home for family and friends to care for.

Eight weeks passed before it was determined that there might be a chance for her *placenta previa* baby to be delivered naturally. However, every precaution was taken when she was in the labor room, just across the hall from the delivery room. The emergency team was on hand. The doctors kept a very close watch on her, but in spite of all that was done she began to hemorrhage when the membrane was ruptured.

Everyone was alerted to the crisis as she was rushed into the operating room. She cried to her doctor, "I don't want to die!" He answered quickly but not very convincingly, "You probably won't."

Those words echoed in my ears, and my whole being was trembling with fear and concern. I was weeping and praying for her safe delivery and for the health and well-being of the baby too. Just about four or five minutes later, the doctor sent someone out to tell me that he had delivered the baby by Caesarian section and that both mother and baby were suffering from the loss of blood, but he thought everything would be all right.

More prayers of gratitude were offered through tears. About then a nurse came from the delivery room with a baby so blue that it was almost black, and I asked if it was our baby. She said, "Yes, if your baby is the Faulkner baby." She rushed into the elevator and took the baby to the infant intensive care unit and the help of those waiting for her.

When Catherine came from the delivery room, she was

almost a transparent white. Normally, she has very white skin but that day there was no color, no pink in her fingernails, no blush to her cheeks; there was only that transparent white. I was with her constantly during the time she was in the recovery room, still praying and still anxiously concerned while she was being monitored.

The fragile nature of life was very apparent at that time. One minute she was laughing and talking and wanting to make certain that everything possible was being done for the baby, and the next she was lying silent and white while skilled doctors, nurses, and staff gave her their full attention—and her family prayed.

Each day after that experience seemed to bring added health and vigor to both our newest little granddaughter and to her mother. I was never more aware of our dependency upon the power of the Almighty God than at that critical time. I knew everything depended on him and prayed that the doctors would be in complete harmony with his will. I was just as quick to express my feelings of deep humility and gratitude to him.

This little granddaughter that cost so much in faith and prayer must be given a full and complete understanding of the ways she can draw close to God and trust in his goodness and love. And I know she will be.

Babies come into families in many ways. The blessings of God come to sanctify each new addition to a family if there is faith and testimony and a humble heart.

There was never a cuter little boy than the one holding the hand of the temple worker who brought Jeff into the sealing room to be with his parents at that holy altar. If they were all faithful, they could be together for time and all eternity.

I don't know if it was his bright red hair, or that striking contrast against the purity of the white shirt, short pants, bow tie, and knee socks—or perhaps it was his captivating friendliness that struck me. I remember he was talking about butterflies as he smiled at his mother and went directly to her. She enfolded him in her arms until the time came for him to stand in that sacred place with Julie across from him, and his mother and father across from each other. This was a moment longed for and looked forward to with the greatest of anticipation by those witnessing that sealing. All of the promises made there that day were predicated upon the faithfulness of those participants. Promises made there have to do with eternal ties. Those of us watching felt very near to heaven at that moment.

Ordinance work brings one very close to heavenly beings. I remember the naming and blessing of each of my own children, but as a grandmother each of the thirty-six events has brought me many more reflective moments.

My grandson John was given a wonderful blessing when he received his name. He was named for John the Baptist, who loved the Lord; for John the Beloved of the Lord; and for a good and dear friend who had opened his home and heart to the family when his father went to the Midwest to train as an ophthalmologist. The friend was a good example of faithfully living the gospel of Jesus Christ. The name *John* expressed the faith and hope the family had for that baby boy who was so wanted and welcomed as the second son in the family. The first boy had been the first child and John was the sixth child. He came after four daughters in a row. The whole family had every wish for him to follow the ways of the Lord. The name was given by the power of the priesthood as is the pattern, and I felt then as now great gratitude for the blessing of this great sealing power.

Doug's mother, our children's Grandmother Smith, was a blessed grandmother. Each grandchild was regally welcomed into her family circle with appropriate gifts, even down to the new expected first great-grandchild, who was born after her death.

When each grandchild became ready to be baptized into the Church, she saw to it they received a Bible engraved with their name and appropriately inscribed: "With love on your eighth birthday. We sincerely hope that you will find much joy in reading your Bible often. Love, Grandma Winnie and Grandpa Virgil."

Another thing she did without fail came in the ninth year of each grandchild's life. If the grandchild so desired, Grandma Winnie would give him or her a Book of Remembrance with a heritage chart that she would type and then illustrate with pictures.

Not a single grandchild missed the pleasure of playing games with Grandma Winnie. And they didn't win just because they were children, either. She taught them to think and to plan and to win through their own ingenuity and effort. The twenty-fourth of December and the twenty-fourth of July became times of cherished tradition because of this illustrious grandmother— a big dinner party, a family program, and tributes to the life of the Savior came at Christmas. On the twenty-fourth of July she honored our pioneer ancestors to give our grandchildren added testimony and understanding of the glorious gospel she loved and proclaimed. No one could ever have been more proud over any accomplishment or righteous endeavor than she was of her grandchildren.

We have not codified our response to these special days in our children's and in our grandchildren's lives, but we have always proudly participated in the services. In fact, sometimes we have become speakers or performers.

Our granddaughter Barbara could hardly wait for her eighth birthday. She knew that the bishop would want her to have her own individual baptismal service. Even before that day she asked to talk with her father so that she could explain exactly what she hoped would take place. He was impressed with the deep thought she had given the meeting. She wanted all four of her grandparents to participate by giving either a prayer or a message regarding baptism and the gift of the Holy Ghost. Her father agreed with every plan she suggested. He encouraged her to call and invite her grandparents to participate with her.

It was just as she had hoped; they were all pleased and happy to respond to her request. She then called all of her aunts, uncles, and cousins and invited them to be present for her baptism. Next, she called her Primary teacher and the Primary presidency. Last she asked her brother if he would sing a duet with her just before her father gave the final message of the service. He did. That tall, handsome brother knelt beside his sister and they harmonized in their songs of praise. We wept. What a very special privilege it was just to be present and to partake of that spiritual feast. The refreshments served were a token effort after the nourishment given to our spirits.

Recently we participated in the confirmation of our grand-son Scott. The meeting was deeply moving. First, of course, there was the prayer of confirmation. Just to look at the circle grow larger and larger as the grandfather, uncles, and ward leaders gathered to place their hands on his head and confirm him a member of the Church was inspirational.

It was when Scott stood and for the first time bore his testi-mony that our eyes filled with tears. When he sat down he said, "That was really scary." His mother then spoke of her grati-tude. His father stood, too, and expressed his appreciation for the bonds of brotherhood he felt in the ward and for the strong family bonds as well which had added so much to his life. He spoke of some activities that members of the family had ini-tiated which built bridges of friendship and love by continued attentiveness.

Then my husband arose. "It is important to remember," he told us all, "that this boy would not be here today receiving his Church membership had it not been for the intervention of the Lord four years ago when this newest member of the Church was a four-year-old boy." He explained that Scott had been walking in the barnyard with his grandfather and his father when without warning the wind blew the loose barn door and toppled it over onto the child. Badly hurt, he had received a blessing. "Those present had the right to call upon the Lord for a blessing," he said, "and now look at him. He is a fine, strapping young man."

My husband reminded us that it was only through the power of the Lord that Scott was there with us at all. His worthiness of baptism and confirmation made that a particularly significant event. Douglas was speaking of the Lord's love and direction from the innermost wellspring of his own heart. There was a hush in the building, and I felt my own understanding of the profound nature of human relations with the divine grow during that meeting.

We were glad that the Lord had spared the life of our grand-son. That time together enriched us all.

Scott's journal entry for that day read, "I just got baptized by immersion. I got baptized by my dad. I was scared—a lot. But, I was very happy too. David was there and Sarah and Steven and Brian. Of course my mom was, and my dad and my grandpas and grandmas.'' (He went on to name all the members of the extended family and his friends and Primary teacher and the presidency.) Then he added, ''I am clean of my sins.''

It was a time of new beginnings.

Once while visiting in Hawaii, I met with a Relief Society stake board for lunch. I asked each member of the board to share some thought about her work in Relief Society. One woman said she had been called as the missionary/activation board member. She was blessed because she had always wanted to be a missionary. She remembered that when she was a little girl her grandmother had only a grass home, but one room of it was saved for the missionaries when they came by. The missionaries always had the best food the family had to offer. Often the family would go without. Each time this sister looked into that room saved for the missionaries she determined that one day she would go into the mission field and have the best room and the best food. As she grew older she grew also in admiration for her grandmother, whose faith was so strong that she not only knew when the servants of God would come but would also be prepared for them. There were many years before the Relief Society sister realized that blessings had come to the family because of her grandmother. The Relief Society board member was delighted to serve the Lord, and her faith and testimony had greatly increased because of her calling.

I thought of her devotion when lifelong friends received a mission call to go to Nova Scotia. At their farewell, the children still at home (three out of their thirteen) participated in the sacrament service with them. Each member of the family took a facet of the premortal, mortal, or eternal life of Christ and told of the principle of love that directed him. All of their family members there sang the touching song about Jesus, ''I Heard Him Come.'' When these friends came to Provo to attend the Missionary Training Center, they came early enough to spend about one week with each of their children who lived in the area. Then one daughter, their eldest child, had a missionary shower for them. She had planned and organized it so that all of the grandchildren could participate. Each grandchild gave them first a gift of love. To do that each grandchild had memorized a scripture on love. One tiny child recited only, "Jesus wept." But each one gave something of love from the life or words of Jesus. Twenty-five of their forty-four grandchildren were present for that occasion. Then each grandchild gave them a gift of warmth: one gave gloves, another hats, another mufflers, and so on. The children and the grandchildren wanted to do their part for their grandparents who had lived the gospel principles and had supported their children as they served in their mission fields.

Missionary work is a very sacred work, and many families save all their lives in order to send a child into the mission field. We have just recently sent our first grandson on a mission. I know that he was prepared well in his home. I know that he was earnest in his study with his father and mother during those last few months before he went out. But something he said at his departure set my heart aglow.

As we stood by him at the airport chatting and smiling and wishing him well, he turned to me and said, "Well, Grandma, how does it seem for you to come to the airport to see me off? All through the years I have come down to see you go on your Church assignments, and now it is my turn to go."

He kissed me and boarded the flight. The jetway was retracted and the plane moved from the building. Soon under its own power it headed toward the runway. There it sat poised like a giant bird filled with cargo and passengers, one of whom was so precious to me. Shortly it rolled forward and its nose lifted by jet power; then it was airborne.

His words reverberated in my mind and found a place deep within my heart. Had I really made a difference in his life? Paul's words came to mind: "Be thou an example of the believer, in word, in conversation, in charity, in spirit, in faith, in purity" (1 Timothy 4:12). Could it possibly be said of my fine young grandson what the Apostle Paul said of Timothy, "I call to remembrance the unfeigned faith that is in thee, which dwelt first in thy grandmother Lois, and thy mother Eunice; and I am persuaded that [is] in thee also" (2 Timothy 1:5).

I hoped he would have good things to remember to sustain

him while he served his mission. Sometimes one's service is not received with an open heart and mind; I had found that as a Relief Society president.

Growth in understanding and living of the gospel is never-ending. All that one learns in giving service becomes useful in the next act of service. All that one learns shapes each day's new experience.

When ye are in the service of your fellow beings ye are only in the service of your God.

—Mosiah 2:17

CHAPTER TWELVE

Growing Through Community Service

It is important to remember that being a grandmother does not mean the end of one's personal productive life. It is not the sole role a woman will perform from the moment her child gives birth to a grandchild until the end of mortality. Measured in moments spent it can only be a small fraction of one's time.

What happens to a grandmother in her other moments, hours, days, weeks, months, years? She cannot hover over her children and their children; the scriptures tell us there is power within us to do much good in the world, too.

My life has always been centered on my religious faith and in my family responsibilities. It has been a good anchor, and I would choose those firm foundation stones again and again.

There is a very "Mormon" word frequently used to describe the approach the faithful servant takes to the work of the Lord. When one is called and set apart for service in the Church, he or she is almost always admonished to *magnify* the calling so that the service may be a blessing to those for whom one works.

It is because of that concept that I have found each year of my life to be richer and fuller than the year before.

"Magnifying" my responsibilities as a mother and then as a grandmother has made my family opportunities greater in both number and magnitude. More important, it has offered innumerable challenges and important, often unexpected possibilities for enriching my life and the lives of my loved ones.

I am aware that opening our home to many who have been alone in the world lightened my work load and opened up minutes and hours to special experiences I could share with my children.

Aunt Martha came to stay with us in Salt Lake City, not because there weren't other members of the family but because she wanted to do genealogical research and temple work and volunteer work at the Primary Children's Hospital. She thought about me and my large family and knew that she could help me if I enjoyed having her live in our home. She was more helpful than "Mr. Clean." Aunt Martha was up early and had household tasks done every day before she left to do all of the things that added interest to her life. When she came home she might nap for a few minutes but then was up and full of energy until late in the evening. Dishes were cleared from the table and washed almost before the family was through eating. She established a weekly routine of cleaning that was completed regularly. Her time was made available to play with or read to the children. I believe everybody needs an Aunt Martha, and I know there could be happier families if the many Aunt Marthas only knew that people needed them.

In the years my children were in school I worked long and hard in the PTA trying to strengthen the ties between home and school to make a better learning situation for all children. Service in the Church organizations and in the community brought new ideas and interesting people into our home. There is no question in my mind but that these service involvements enabled us all to see things from a little broader perspective than before.

But the necessary cares of a young and growing family keep the mother in closer range. In a way those years were a training ground for me. I learned skills that later in my life were to expand my horizons beyond my wildest childhood dreams.

For one thing, I learned to respond to a Church calling, believing in its value and confident that the work was significant. When I was called to serve as general president of the Relief Society I was already a grandmother.

Suddenly, my world no longer began and ended within the valley of the Great Salt Lake. In a brief moment my responsibilities were expanded to include all of the women of the Church, and within months I was to discover that they lived all over the world.

Certainly my vision expanded as to who belonged to the sisterhood known as Relief Society. It was all women who believed in the Lord Jesus Christ and the restoration of his Gospel. And through that gospel it meant that I must take very seriously the fact that all the women of the world were sisters. This was a growing experience for me.

My trip to the Far East was fascinating. I thank each woman who invited me into her home so that I might know more of the way life is lived there. One delightful Japanese child watched me wash my hands at their basin, and she called to her mother, "She knows how to use our basin!" We laughed together because we both understood the child's amazement.

In Norway I visited lovely homes and then went to see where the elderly were living in government-operated institutions. Each phase of life is given full consideration. Those that were there told us how pleased they were first to visit and attend social functions, then to come for weekends until they felt the need to be there in the facility for the aged all the time. They liked the options that were theirs.

I saw the old and the young, the rich and the poor, the single and the married people as I traveled the world.

But interestingly enough it was not my visits as general president that touched me most deeply and awakened most surely in my heart an appreciation for all of God's children. It was something that happened right here at home. My youngest daughter married a fine young Mexican whom she had known throughout her junior and senior high school years.

When Hector and Sherilynn decided to marry, I felt the reservations that come about the problems of joining two cultural traditions in one family circle. They had a lot of things in common besides their love. They had two strong family support systems. They had the gospel. They had strong traditions for continued education. These are the things that allow the intellect to cut through prejudice and practice and follow eternal guidelines. But nothing fully erases the fact that people do have differences in their cultural traditions, and these differences can hurt.

But what I have come to realize is that these differences can be marvelously exhilarating, and they can shed wonderful new rays of light and excitement in a home determined to make a successful adjustment.

I had been growing in my appreciation of other cultural heritages since before I was the general president. When I was a member of the general board of Relief Society, we had inaugurated a series of lessons on the various countries of the world. After becoming the general president I had traveled to many countries.

There is no question but that the personal dimension had a tremendous impact on me. In particular I remember a bridal shower held for Sherilynn and Hector by the Alba family. It was held in the cultural hall of a ward meetinghouse. Family members and friends alike came to honor them. The cultural hall was decorated with piñatas and brightly colored paper flowers. We could hear the mariachis playing festive music even before we entered the room. The tables were arranged around the outside of the room, covered with cloths of orange, yellow, and red. The food was superb: enchiladas, rice, beans, tacos, and bunualos. I never really knew before that shower that I was a fan of Mexican food, but no one could resist the delicious flavors and textures. As soon as the guests were served dinner the *Ballet Folklorico* dancing began. I will always remember it because it was beautifully costumed and performed and even more because of the feet of the little children who were watching. They were all tapping their toes and laughing and finally twirling to the music. No one stopped them. The Mexicans seemed to love to watch the children having such a good time.

I noted and felt the warmth of this great family that night. There was joy in the coming nuptials. The feeling of complete celebration pervaded the whole evening.

Since their marriage I have come to appreciate the depth of Hector's commitment as a husband and father. I have come to understand that my daughter is blessed by a whole cultural tradition of warmth and love.

In many ways all of us may bless our own lives by coming to a greater appreciation and understanding of other peoples in the world. Perhaps we should all begin with a little study. Besides the lectures and books of other years, we now have films and videos available which allow us to hear and to see and to learn much of another country.

In addition there are opportunities for service. In Utah there is a large refugee population from Southeast Asia, many of whom need to learn to speak English. Volunteers are needed.

It is a matter of national disgrace that migrant workers and their children have extremely limited opportunity for schooling. Such problems would yield to determined efforts to improve the situation by people who loved others in the pattern given by the Savior.

Many of our friends have been called to serve among peoples of other lands in teaching the gospel.

Many of us visit other countries on vacations—maybe only once in a lifetime—but if we go looking for the opportunities to share and to appreciate what we find there we will be blessed. It is very important whether at home or abroad to eradicate from our minds and hearts the short-sighted negative comparisons between our way of life and the way others live.

There are many ways to look at the world, and they all add delight to our lives. There are many ways to love and many ways to appreciate individuals, and they all add richness to our lives.

In the course of my ten years of service as the general president of the Relief Society, many additional vistas were opened to my mind and in the course of service my heart learned to love in new and better ways.

My years were the years in which the whole nation and to some degree the whole world sought to re-examine the role of women. Every cherished guideline for a woman's life has come under scrutiny—sometimes quite unfriendly scrutiny. The battle was thrust upon the Relief Society by confrontations over the ERA and other initiatives. The questions raised are still being debated and redefined, and the face of society is being reshaped.

I have never had a more extraordinary experience in my life than service as general president. I have grown in many, many ways, not the least of which is my greatly expanded under-standing of the vast diversity of circumstances in which women live their lives—both grandmothers and non-grandmothers, single and married, rich and poor.

Almost always my interaction with people has left me an improved person. As my understanding of human suffering and struggle has grown, I have grown.

I shall always remember the stake Relief Society president who came into my office and told me that as a child she had never known a happy day until her grandmother took her to the Mormon church. She said it was just as if a light had been turned on in her life. Just being there made her happy. She looked forward to each meeting she could attend. Then her mother told her that they were going to move away. The Relief Society president told me that she began to cry. Her mother said, "Don't cry, at least until you see the place where we are going to live."

Their new house was right next door to the Mormon chapel. She told me that she was able to go to two Sunday School meet-ings, to two Primary meetings, and to two sacrament services every week.

I marveled at her, beginning with such an unhappy start in life and becoming the stake Relief Society president. But she explained that she had been guided and blessed right up to the moment she found a wonderful member of the Church to marry and that her married life was one of complete happiness and selfless love.

A sister blind from birth came into my office with a most positive attitude. Her marriage had ended in divorce, but her life was filled with interesting and progressive activities. It was her sweet manner and kindness that helped me to realize a little more the importance of directing ourselves in happy ways.

I think also of a single woman who was called to work with a Young Adult Relief Society group. Her health was not the best, but because of her determined attitude the girls under her leadership were fascinated by the depth of her thinking.

As my experiences on national committees have led me to an in-depth study of families, economic opportunities for women, national laws and initiatives, and the problems of aging, I have become aware of many good programs which have been started by concerned citizens. Dr. Russell B. Clark was concerned enough to sponsor an essay contest at Brigham Young University for the purpose of allowing the young and the old to explore some of the positive aspects of growing older. He wanted all of us to know that life does not end with the passing of youth but that our later years should be a productive and rewarding part of our lives, something to look forward to. He quotes Robert Browning's statement that "the best is yet to be."

It is very pleasant to see that young children can become very positively involved with older people when they are given a motive. They learn that they want to "be a grandma, just like Grandma Payne" or that "old people are so neat . . . , they make me feel good. They tell me stories . . . and I learn lots from them. . . . They can learn from me too."

Orem, Utah, has developed a program to bring together the old, the young, the child, the teenager, the newly married, the longtime married, the parent, the grandparent, and the single. Everyone is to be a part of their Family City, USA. They really want to be just exactly that, a city that includes every member of the family. They work to be together in open theater programs and activities. Grandmothers can become involved in whatever area of personal interest brings forth in them the commitment for a successful venture.

Every city and state has some kind of volunteer program of which we can be a part.

Currently I am serving as the president of the Utah chapter of the National Committee for the Prevention of Child Abuse. It is a very sobering assignment. As far as I am concerned there should be no child abuse at all. I understand the problems as defined by scholarly study, and these studies help shape responses to the problems.

In our state we are finding that society can take a number of valuable initiatives. We can give family counseling. We can provide crisis centers to remove children from potential violence. We can offer in-house training for new mothers to give them and new fathers a better understanding of the new child and its ways. We can support in-home demonstrations to show parents how they might use play time to enrich their personal relationships with their children.

The point is that there is no problem for which there can never be a solution. It takes creative imagination and great dedication, but we can discover new ways of dealing with this and its related problems.

Perhaps it is as Goethe observed: "It is only necessary to grow old to become more charitable and even indulgent. I see no fault committed by others that I have not committed myself."

It has long been my personal conviction that all we have learned in our families and in our churches is designed to prepare us for continued contribution in society. Sometimes that contribution will come when we are part of an organized effort. Sometimes it will mean initiating a new response to help solve a difficult problem. Sometimes it will mean a personal response to a private need in the family, among friends, or of a neighbor.

When the Lord said to Lehi's children, "Be not weary in well doing," he was suggesting the best possible trail for our last years. Those years come while we are grandmothers. We need to remember this.

It is said that Thomas A. Edison's wife used to complain that Thomas worked too hard and needed a rest. "You must forget about work and go on a vacation," she declared.

"But where would I go?" he asked.

She replied very simply, "Just decide where you'd rather be more than anywhere else on earth, and then go there."

"Very well," promised Edison. "I will go there tomorrow." The next morning he went back to work in his laboratory.

When I was serving on a national committee for the aging, I talked with a number of older people. Their eyesight was going and their health was failing. "What," they were asked, "could society do for you that would make you most happy?"

"Just help us be part of the mainstream of society," they said. "Let us help solve the problems we face in our communities. Let us help serve those among us with great needs."

I suspect that is the way I want it because that is the only way I know to keep growing.

Every neighborhood and each community has service needs to be met by willing workers. Every church needs the tireless work of the pioneer.

Observing an evergreen tree in springtime when new growth appears, it is with some fascination that one notices new shoots of green have pushed out of the older and darker green branches and needles. This soft, delicate green is an extension of the existing structure of the tree. It comes forth very naturally.

Growth that comes to grandmothers through continued service is just such growth. It softens and it extends. It is wonderful.

Epilogue

The new combined labor and delivery room at the LDS Hospital in Salt Lake City is not much like the room in that hospital in which I gave birth to my seven children. I had spent the morning there with my youngest daughter talking and laughing with her and waiting. When I had waited for my first grandchild it had been in a much more austere setting. Then I was separated from my daughter and there was no sharing with her the long waiting period.

But now that I was waiting for the birth of my thirty-sixth grandchild, there was a much more friendly atmosphere. Sherilynn played games with us. I was there with her husband, her father, and her mother- and father-in-law. Everybody was in a party mood.

I was surprised at the changes that had taken place from the time of my first delivery until this one. Sherilynn was consulted on every procedure that was to take place. She was given as much or as little medication as she wanted. No one was telling her what was right or wrong for her. She was making the decisions.

When she complained that the labor pains were more intense than the monitors indicated she was assured that she alone could really tell them about the intensity of the pain. The machine could only measure accurately the length of the contraction. Her every request was given full consideration and she was to control the situation. This was to be her fourth child. Those attending her were deferential. They assumed she knew something of what was about to happen.

When it was time for the baby to be born, the doctor asked her visitors to leave. Sherilynn said, "I think Mother should stay and watch the delivery of this baby. She has never watched a baby being born, not even any of her own." The doctor said, "She is welcome to stay if she wants to." His answer was also a question. I told him the only hospital procedure I had ever watched was a cornea transplant. He laughed, said it was not the same, and then asked if I wanted to stay. I said I did, so the nurse immediately left the room and came back with a gown for me.

In the meantime the bed was disassembled and made into a delivery table. No rushing from one location to another. It was just minutes before he said, "Here comes the baby. See its little head?" Then, after one more push the baby's whole head was in his skilled hands and he was suctioning out the baby's mouth as he helped the shoulders and the rest of the body come from its mother. I was fascinated.

The baby's first cry was a thrill to hear. The knowledge that the baby so long awaited had finally come and that all was well was exciting. The baby was wrapped in a warm cloth and handed first to its mother and father. Then they let me hold her. I thrilled at the miracle I had just witnessed. I *had* just witnessed it, and yet I could not comprehend the divine nature of the occurrence. It was accomplished by a power that brought me to humble reverence. Every baby is a miracle wrought by God with a little help from a man and a woman. But this birth I had seen. It had taken place before my very eyes and it was my own daughter's child. It was, with only a little leap, bone of my bone and flesh of my flesh.

Hector left to share the good news with the other waiting grandparents.

There were tears of tenderness as I looked toward my youngest daughter and her newborn child.

This infant girl was the thirty-sixth grandchild in my family, but the feeling of absolute awe had not diminished. I asked the doctor when one gets over this overwhelming feeling of wonder at the birth of a child.

"I don't know," he said quite seriously. "You'll have to ask someone else. I've only delivered a few thousand babies and it hasn't happened to me yet."

Holding the child so newly come from heaven was like a glimpse into that distant place. I wept. Sherilynn did too. She said, "Mother, I needed to have you here. You have been through this, too, and I knew if you were with me I would be fine."

I felt a little as I did when I saw my grandmother throw back her head and laugh with the sheer delight of seeing a window full of children watching the newborn in Wyoming so many years ago.

In a very real way I thought, *This is the most wonderful of all babies I have ever known.* I had participated in the event—at least I had watched it up close and felt Sherilynn's confidence because I was there.

Being a grandmother goes on. And I am glad because I am just now beginning to understand the rhythm of it. I wonder what lies ahead for me and for my children and grandchildren. I guess I am glad I do not know all of the details. There is mercy in struggling through one problem at a time.

I am quite sure of one thing: I still have much to learn.

Dr. Joshua Liebman writes: "The great thing is that as long as we live we have the privilege of growing. We can learn new skills, engage in new kinds of work, devote ourselves to new causes, make new friends. Accepting then the truth that we are capable in some directions and limited in others, that genius is rare, that mediocrity is the portion of most of us, let us remember that we can and must change ourselves. Until the day of our death we can grow. We can tap hidden resources in our makeup." (Joshua Liebman, *Getting the Most Out of Our Lives* [AMG Publishers, 1976].)

I am very certain of this now.

In the great diversity of human experience which comes with the years and is compounded with growing families, there is constant and continuing growth. It may be the diminishing number of years or it may be the burgeoning number of opportunities, but my years as a grandmother seem to be very full— of opportunity, of challenge, and of personal growth.

Index